SCIENCE **T**ECHNOLOGY **E**NGINEERING **M**ATH

STEM QUEST

ASTONISHING ATOMS
AND
MATTER MAYHEM

BARRON'S

First edition for the United States and Canada published in 2018 by Barron's Educational Series, Inc.

All inquiries should be addressed to:
Barron's Educational Series, Inc.
250 Wireless Boulevard
Hauppauge, NY 11788
www.barronseduc.com

Executive editor: Selina Wood
Managing art editor: Dani Lurie
Design: Claire Barber
Illustrator: Annika Brandow
Picture research: Steve Behan
Production: Emma Smart
Editorial consultant: Jack Challoner

ISBN: 978-1-4380-1136-3

Library of Congress Control Number: 2017959664

Date of Manufacture: May 2018
Printed by Oriental Press, Jebel Ali, Dubai, U.A.E.

9 8 7 6 5 4 3 2 1

AUTHOR
Colin Stuart

Colin Stuart is a science speaker and author who has talked about the wonders of the universe to well over a quarter of a million people. His books have sold over 100,000 copies worldwide and he has written over 150 popular science articles. He is a Fellow of the Royal Astronomical Society.

For Edith, Stanley, Max, and Joshua.

STEM EDITORIAL CONSULTANT
Georgette Yakman

Georgette Yakman is the founding researcher and creator of the integrative STEAM framework with degrees in Integrated STEM Education, Technology, and Fashion Design. She is the CEO of STEAM Education and works in over 20 countries offering educational professional development courses and consulting as an international policy advisor.

ILLUSTRATOR
Annika Brandow

Annika Brandow is an artist specializing in character illustration and illustrated typography. Her work spans advertising, publishing, and online. She loves the challenge of making difficult topics fun and easily digestible through illustration.

The publishers would like to thank the following sources for their kind permission to reproduce the pictures in the book.

9. Nationalmuseum, Stockholm via Wikimedia Commons, 13. Private Collection, 17. Public Domain, 18. GL Archive/Alamy Stock Photo, 19. ITV/REX/Shutterstock, 21-22. Public Domain, 23. Bob Daugherty/AP/REX/Shutterstock, 24. Public Domain, 27. Getty Images, 29. Universal History Archive/UIG via Getty Images, 31. Wellcome Library, London, 32. Science Photo Library, 35. Wellcome Library, London, 37, Public Domain, 39. NASA, 40-53. Public Domain, 61. Photogravure Meisenbach Riffarth & Co. Leipzig via Wikimedia Common, 63. National Maritime Museum, Greenwich, London, 65. Public Domain, 66. CORBIS/Corbis via Getty Images, 68. Smithsonian Institution, 70. Public Domain, 72. Wellcome Library, London, 74. Sam Ogden/Whitehead Institute Jaenisch, 75. Topfoto.co.uk

Every effort has been made to acknowledge correctly and contact the source and/or copyright holder of each picture, and Carlton Books apologizes for any unintentional errors or omissions, which will be corrected in future editions of this book.

Adult supervision is recommended for all activities.

SCIENCE TECHNOLOGY ENGINEERING MATH

STEM QUEST

ASTONISHING ATOMS AND MATTER MAYHEM

Colin Stuart

BARRON'S

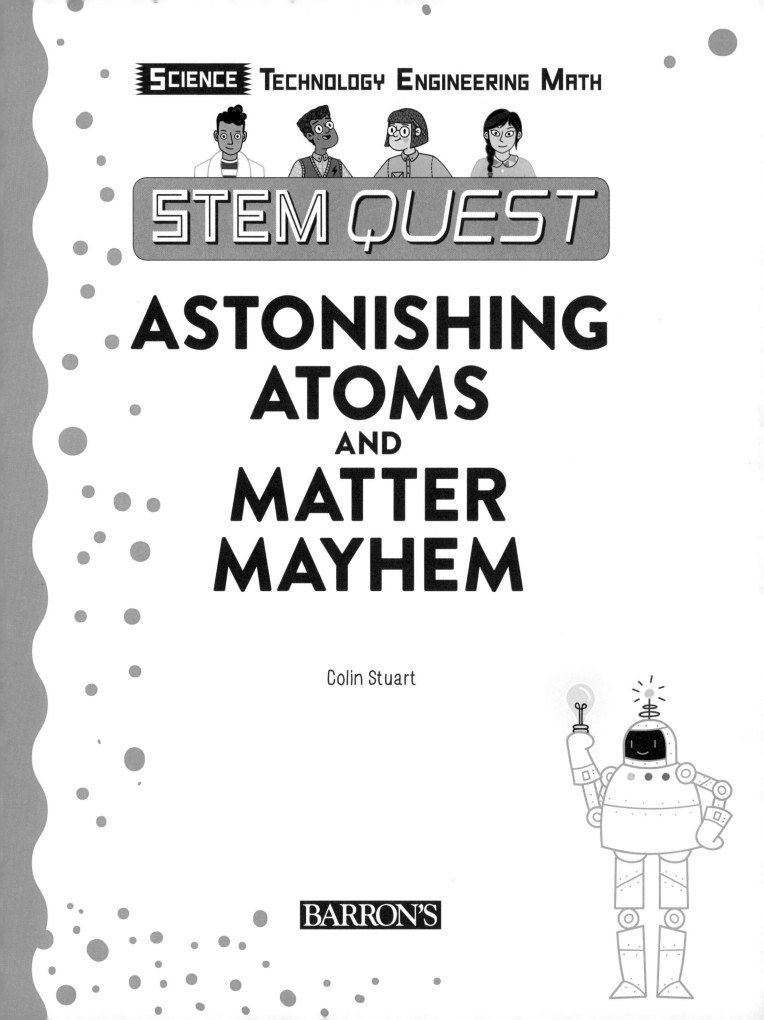

CONTENTS

Biology	Chemistry	Physics	Earth and Space Sciences	Biochemistry	Biomedicine	Biotechnology

WELCOME TO STEM QUEST!

We're the **STEM Squad**, and we'd like to introduce you to the wonderful world of STEM: **Science, Technology, Engineering,** and **Math**. The **STEM Quest** series has a book on each of these fascinating subjects, and we are here to guide you through them. STEM learning gives you real-life examples and experiments to help you relate these subjects to the world around you. We hope you will discover that no matter who you are, you can be whatever you want to be: a scientist, an engineer, a technologist, or a mathematician. Let's take a closer look...

SCIENCE

In science you investigate the world around you.

Carlos and Ella

Super scientist **Carlos** is an expert on supernovas, gravity, and bacteria. **Ella** is Carlos's lab assistant. Carlos is planning a trip to the Amazon rain forest where Ella can collect, organize, and store data!

TECHNOLOGY

In technology you develop products and gadgets to improve our world.

Lewis and Violet

Top techy **Lewis** dreams of being on the first spaceship to Mars. Gadget genius **Violet** was built by Lewis from recycled trash.

ENGINEERING

In engineering you solve problems to create extraordinary structures and machines.

Olive and Clark

Olive is an incredible engineer who built her first skyscraper (out of dog biscuits) at the age of three. **Clark** was discovered by Olive on a trip to the pyramids of Giza.

MATH

In math you explore numbers, measurements and shapes.

Sophie and Pierre

Math wizard **Sophie** impressed her class by working out the ratio of popcorn-lovers to doughnut-munchers. **Pierre** is Sophie's computer backup. His computer skills are helping to unlock the mystery of prime numbers.

SCIENCE IS WHAT HAPPENS WHEN CURIOUS PEOPLE ASK QUESTIONS.

Science is the study of the world around us. It's all about trying to understand how the earth and the universe work. Science is at the heart of our modern life, from the latest medicine and the newest smartphone to looking for life on other planets and protecting the oceans from pollution. Science is not just a collection of facts and inventions—it is a way of thinking. Scientists don't take someone else's word for something. They make predictions and perform experiments to try to figure out what is really going on. There are many different branches of science. Let's explore them:

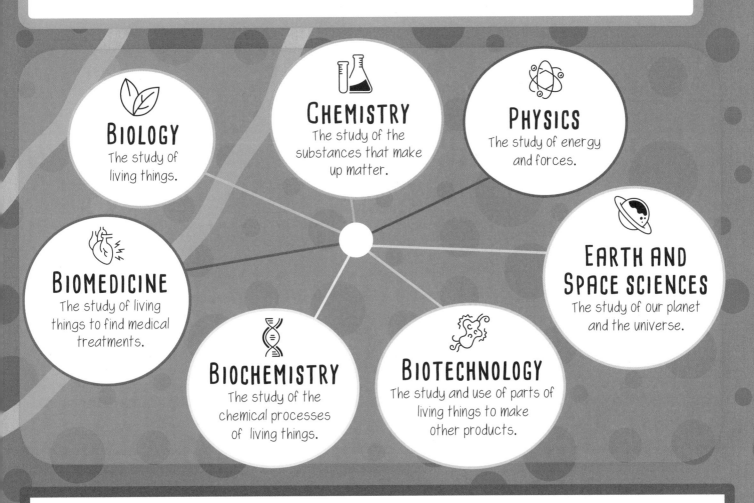

BIOLOGY
The study of living things.

CHEMISTRY
The study of the substances that make up matter.

PHYSICS
The study of energy and forces.

BIOMEDICINE
The study of living things to find medical treatments.

BIOCHEMISTRY
The study of the chemical processes of living things.

BIOTECHNOLOGY
The study and use of parts of living things to make other products.

EARTH AND SPACE SCIENCES
The study of our planet and the universe.

A lot of people don't realize that they are being scientists all the time in their everyday lives. Have you ever tried changing the time your alarm goes off to see if it makes a difference in how awake you feel in the morning? That's an experiment. Have you ever tried walking a different route to a friend's house to see if it is quicker? That's an experiment, too.
You're already a scientist!

In this book you're going to explore what science has told us about the way the world works. There are lots of activities and experiments for you to try so that you can see for yourself how amazing science is. Could you be a scientist who one day cracks some of our biggest mysteries? With hard work and determination, there is absolutely no reason why you can't.
Dream big, and good luck!

PLANTS

Plants are some of the most important living things on Earth. Not only do they give us food to eat, but they also make lots of oxygen for us to breathe.

petal
flower
nectar
leaf

WHAT'S GOING ON?

PARTS OF A FLOWER

The roots absorb water and **nutrients** from the soil. The stem transports water to the leaves. Leaves convert sunlight into **energy** so the plant can grow. Some flowering plants have brightly-colored petals and sugary **nectar** that attract insects. Flowers also contain powdery grains called **pollen**. Insects carry the pollen from one flower to another. If pollen lands on a flower of the same type, it can form a seed and grow into a new plant.

stem

root

what's the BIG idea?

PHOTOSYNTHESIS

Photosynthesis is the way in which a plant makes its own food. A green substance in the leaves called chlorophyll traps energy from sunlight. The **cells** in the leaves use this energy to turn **carbon dioxide** (from the air) and water into **oxygen** and a type of sugar called glucose, which it uses as food.

sunlight
+
carbon dioxide
+
water

photosynthesis

glucose
+
oxygen

LEAF LIGHT TEST!

Plants need several things to survive, including light, water, and nutrients. Let's explore how important light is to a plant.

YOU WILL NEED:

- ✔ A healthy houseplant or outside plant with big leaves (and permission to damage a handful of leaves)
- ✔ A sunny spot
- ✔ Clear plastic wrap
- ✔ Aluminum foil
- ✔ Paper
- ✔ Mesh or netting
- ✔ Paperclips

1. Put the plant in a sunny spot where you can leave it for 7–10 days.

2. Carefully cover two separate leaves with a piece of plastic wrap and attach with paperclips.

3. Repeat this step for each of the coverings: foil, paper, mesh (or netting). Do not pinch the leaves or stems.

4. Over the next few days, check the covered leaves and make notes of any changes to them.

5. After 10 days, check and compare your results for each type of covering.

6. Compare each couple of leaves with the same covering. If there are similar changes you'll know it's because of the covering.

HOW DOES IT WORK?

Did you find that some of the leaves began to fade and lose their green color? Think about why this is happening and which of the coverings blocked the sun's light the most. Which covering affected the leaves the fastest? Did any of the coverings become warm in sunlight and harm a leaf by heating it?

WHO WAS LINNEAUS?

Carl Linneaus (1707–1778) was a Swedish botanist—a scientist who studies plants. He came up with the way we order and name different plants and animals.

IN FACT...

390,000 DIFFERENT PLANTS

Scientists know about almost half a million different **species** (types) of plants and are finding new ones all the time. Plants grow on every continent on Earth (even Antarctica!). They range from trees, grass, ferns, moss, and vegetables, and they all make their food in the same way.

AMAZING ANIMALS

Scientists have discovered over one and a half million species (or types) of animals on our planet so far, and they are discovering around 10,000 more every single year!

WHAT'S GOING ON?

WHAT IS AN ANIMAL?

All organisms (living things) belong to one of six groups called kingdoms. The kingdoms are **1)** plants **2)** fungi **3)** animals and also **4)** archaebacteria **5)** eubacteria and **6)** protista, which are types of microscopic living things. A group within a kingdom is called a phylum. Humans belong to the phylum called chordata. They are in the class called mammals.

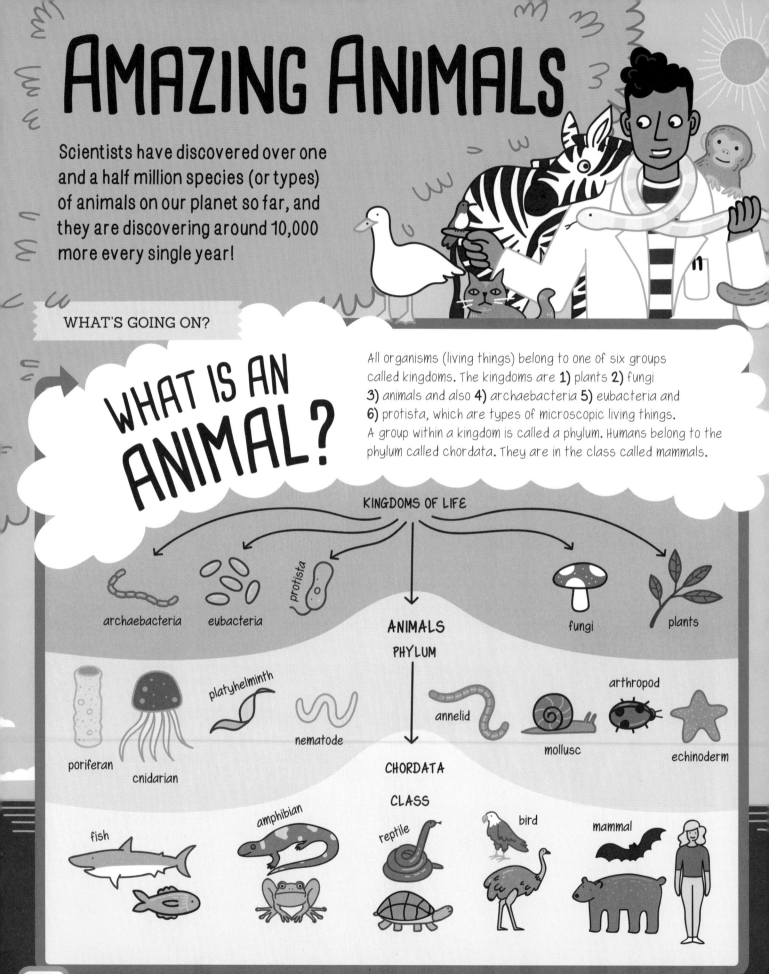

KINGDOMS OF LIFE

archaebacteria eubacteria protista **ANIMALS** fungi plants

PHYLUM

poriferan cnidarian platyhelminth nematode annelid mollusc arthropod echinoderm

CHORDATA

CLASS

fish amphibian reptile bird mammal

CHORDATA CLASSES

Mammals, birds, fish, reptiles, and amphibians belong to the chordata phylum—these are animals with backbones. The major difference between them is how they **reproduce**. Most mammals give birth to live young rather than lay eggs, for instance, and they feed their babies milk.

WHAT'S GOING ON?

WHAT MAKES SOMETHING ALIVE?

A rabbit is clearly alive, but a rock isn't. What separates living things from non-living objects? There are seven key characteristics that living things possess.

1) RESPIRATION
(the ability to process food to release energy)

2) GROWTH
(the ability to grow)

3) EXCRETION
(the ability to get rid of waste products)

4) MOVEMENT
(the ability to move)

5) SENSITIVITY
(the ability to gather information about its surroundings)

6) REPRODUCTION
(the ability to produce young)

7) NUTRITION
(the ability to absorb and digest nutrients from its surroundings)

---

what's the BIG idea?

EXTINCTION?

Ninety-nine percent of the species that have lived on Earth are no longer alive. If the last animal of a species dies, we say that the species has become extinct. Scientists think that the rate of extinction could be well over 10,000 species a year. Extinction is a natural process, but human action, such as hunting or destruction of the species' environments, has caused many species to die out. The flightless dodo bird was famously made extinct through hunting by the year 1662.

The dodo bird

FOOD WEBS

We eat a balance of foods because our bodies need energy to work properly. But where does that energy come from? It's been on quite a remarkable journey!

WHAT'S GOING ON?

EATING SUNSHINE

It all starts with the sun. Plants use the sun's energy, as well as water and nutrients from the earth, to make their own food. When plants are eaten, either by us or by other animals, the energy is passed on. Eating food that comes from animals is another way for us to get this energy. We are all eating sunshine!

what's the BIG idea?

CHAINS AND WEBS

You can draw a chain of energy starting with the sun and ending up with a human. These links make up a food chain. A series of chains combined together to show how energy is transferred in an animal community is called a food web.

FOOD CHAIN

FOOD WEB

PRODUCERS AND CONSUMERS

Plants are called producers because they produce their own energy from sunlight. Animals are called consumers because they eat plants and other animals.

consumer

producer

WHO WAS AL-JAHIZ?

Al-Jahiz (776–868 A.D.) was a writer from Iraq, who was one of the first people to write about the idea of food chains—that animals hunt and are hunted in turn.

YOUR OWN FOOD CHAIN

Write down a list of foods in your favorite breakfast, lunch, or dinner. Now think about what you've eaten today. If it was fruit or vegetables, where did it come from? If it was meat, which animal did it come from and what did that animal eat? You'll find it always traces back to the sun.

PREY AND PREDATOR

Animals that get eaten are called prey. Predators are animals that eat other animals, so you'll find predators at the top of a food web. Many animals are both prey and predators.

what's the BIG idea?

GREENHOUSE EMISSIONS

The earth's human population is growing rapidly, and we all need food to eat. Food production and transport account for nearly a third of our greenhouse gas emissions. These are gases that are causing harm to the **environment** by warming up our planet. Food supply is one of the key problems to solve in the 21st century.

POPULATION CHANGE

Take another look at the food web on the opposite page. What would happen if the number of mice went up or the number of foxes went down? Or what if there was a drought and the wheat was destroyed? Think about this, and you'll see how connected a food web is.

HUMAN BODY

You are an amazing collection of cells, bones, and organs, which are all doing their own special jobs to keep you alive. We don't even notice most of the time!

cranium

humerus

ribs

radius

ulna

pelvis

WHAT'S GOING ON?

YOUR SKELETON

femur

Your skeleton gives your body a framework and protects your body's organs. We are born with 270 bones, but as we grow, some of our bones, including those in our skull and in our pelvis, stick together. So an adult only has 206.

tibia

fibula

what's the BIG idea?

mouth

esophagus

stomach

DIGESTION

Our food goes on a remarkable journey. After you chew it and mix it with saliva in your mouth, it passes down a tube (called the esophagus) to your stomach, where it begins to break down. This continues in the **small intestine**, where the food's nutrients are absorbed into your blood. Your **large intestine** removes water, and eventually expels the waste!

large intestine

small intestine

YOUR EYES

Light enters your eye through your pupil— a small hole in the middle of your eye. A **lens** inside your eye focuses this light onto an area called the **retina** at the back of your eye. The retina turns the light into electrical signals that are sent to your brain, and then you can see!

iris · pupil · retina · signals to brain · lens

YOUR AMAZING EYES!

The human eye is incredible. It has many parts that work together so we can see as much as possible. In this experiment you are going to find out how quickly your eyes respond to your surroundings.

1 Stand in the dark room for a minute with your eyes open.

2 Place the mirror in front of your face.

3 Turn the light switch on.

4 Watch what happens to your pupils.

5 Flick the switch on and off quickly several times, and keep looking at your pupils.

YOU WILL NEED:

✔ A handheld mirror
✔ A dark room with a light switch

HOW DOES IT WORK?

Your pupils can change size depending on the brightness of your surroundings. In dark conditions your pupils get bigger to let in as much light as possible. But when you turn the light on, they suddenly shrink back to their normal size. In bright light your pupil is 2–4 mm across, but in dark conditions it grows to 8 mm wide.

RESPIRATION AND CIRCULATION

You breathe in every three to five seconds. The oxygen that you draw in from the air and into your lungs is transported by your blood throughout your body. This helps to keep you alive. Let's take a look, scientists!

lungs

RED BLOOD CELLS

Tiny sacs in your lungs called alveoli pass the oxygen into your bloodstream where it combines with red blood **cells**. Blood full of oxygen is then carried from the lungs to the heart. The heart pumps the oxygen-rich blood to cells throughout your body.

what's the BIG idea?

capillaries

artery from heart to lungs

vein from lung to heart

heart

VEINS AND ARTERIES

Arteries carry blood away from the heart, while **veins** carry blood back to the heart. Your heart pumps blood to the lungs, where oxygen dissolves into it. The blood returns to the heart, which then pumps it around the rest of the body. Oxygen reaches every cell of your body, and eventually the blood has hardly any left. It returns to the heart to start the cycle over again.

WHO WAS LOGAN?

Myra Adele Logan (1908–1977) was an African-American doctor who was the first woman to perform open heart surgery and was elected to the American College of Surgeons.

WHAT'S GOING ON?

RESPIRATION

Respiration is the chemical process your cells use to turn oxygen and glucose from food into energy. Respiration also produces carbon dioxide and water. The carbon dioxide is transported back into your bloodstream to your lungs where you breathe it out.

glucose + oxygen → carbon dioxide + water + energy

TRY THIS AT HOME

KEEPING PACE

When we run we need more oxygen to power our muscles so our lungs have to work faster and harder. Your heart also works extra hard to get that oxygen around your body. You can explore this for yourself...

YOU WILL NEED:

✔ Space to run around in
✔ A stopwatch

1 Place two fingers (not your thumb) on the veins in your wrist, and find your pulse.

2 Start the stopwatch, and count your pulse for 60 seconds.

3 How many beats did you feel? This is your pulse rate.

4 Now run around for a few minutes.

5 Take your pulse again for one minute. How has it changed?

6 How long does it take for your pulse to return to where it was at the beginning?

17

SUPER CELLS

Cells are the building blocks of living things, including you and me! There are over 37 trillion cells in the human body! Different cells carry out different jobs to keep you alive.

→ what's the **BIG** idea ?

PLANT CELLS OR ANIMAL CELLS?

Animal and plant cells are similar, but not exactly the same. One of the differences is that plant cells have chloroplasts that are used in photosynthesis (see p. 8). A cell wall gives a cell structure and a cell **membrane** acts as a guard, deciding what comes in and out of a cell.

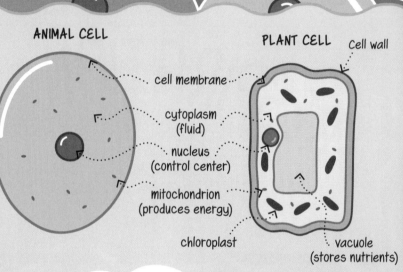

ANIMAL CELL

PLANT CELL — Cell wall

cell membrane

cytoplasm (fluid)

nucleus (control center)

mitochondrion (produces energy)

chloroplast

vacuole (stores nutrients)

IN FACT...

PROKARYOTES

Plant and animal cells are called eukaryotes because they both have a "control center" called a **nucleus**, which is inside of a membrane. The cells of tiny organisms called **bacteria**, however, have no nucleus and are called prokaryotes.

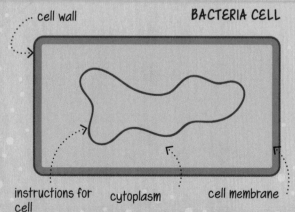

cell wall

BACTERIA CELL

instructions for cell

cytoplasm

cell membrane

WHO WAS HOOKE?

Robert Hooke (1635–1703) was a British scientist who came up with the word "cell" after seeing some plant cells through a microscope he had built.

CELL DIVISION

Your body is constantly making new cells. Your skin cells live for only a couple of weeks before being replaced. In a process called **mitosis**, a cell makes two exact copies of itself called daughter cells.

cell → mitosis → → → daughter cells

WHO WAS LACKS?

Henrietta Lacks (1920–1951) was an African-American cancer patient whose cells were used by scientists (without her permission!) to understand and cure diseases.

TRY THIS AT HOME

CELLS IN ACTION

In this simple experiment with carrots, you can see for yourself how water moves in and out of plant cells through the cell membrane.

1. Stir the salt into one of the glasses of water.

2. Break the carrot in half. Weigh each half and make a note of the weights.

3. Place one half in each glass and leave for 24 hours.

4. What is the difference between the two halves of carrot now? What do you think has happened?

5. Take the carrots out of the water and weigh them. Have they become heavier?

YOU WILL NEED:

✔ A carrot
✔ Two glasses of water
✔ Three tablespoons of salt
✔ A weighing scale

HOW DOES IT WORK?

Water always passes from an area of high **concentration** to an area of low concentration. This is called osmosis. In the glass with the salty water, water inside the carrot cells passed through the cell membranes and the cells shriveled. In the glass with the plain water, the water moved into the carrot's cells and caused them to swell up.

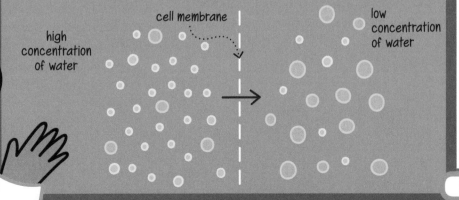

high concentration of water

cell membrane

low concentration of water

GENIUS GENES

Have you ever wondered why people have different colored hair or eyes? Why are some people taller than others? We inherit these traits from our parents through the passing on of genes.

what's the BIG idea?

GENES

Genes are found inside cells. They are instructions for how a cell should behave. Genes are made of a substance called **deoxyribonucleic acid (DNA)**, which is shaped like a twisted ladder —biologists call this shape a **double helix**. Each strand of the ladder is made up of pairs of chemicals called bases.

DNA

base pairs

WHAT'S GOING ON?

CHROMOSOMES

Genes are strung out on long strands of DNA called chromosomes. A normal human has 23 pairs of chromosomes. In each of your pairs there is one chromosome from each of your parents. One particular pair governs whether you are a male or a female. You're a female if you get an X chromosome from each of your parents. You're a male if you get an X from your mom and a Y from your dad.

HUMAN CHROMOSOMES

1 2 3 4 5
6 7 8 9 10 11 12
13 14 15 16 17 18
19 20 21 22 23

XX (FEMALE) XY (MALE)

Very occasionally babies can be born with chromosome combinations other than XX and XY. Klinefelter syndrome is a condition in which a male baby is born with an extra X chromosome. In Turner Syndrome, a female only has one X chromosome, instead of two. Both of these conditions can make the babies unable to have babies naturally later in life. Sometimes a male baby has an extra Y chromosome and a female baby has an extra X chromosome (supermale and metafemale). These babies can grow to be taller than average adults.

KLINEFELTER SYNDROME   TURNER SYNDROME   SUPERMALE   METAFEMALE

XX   XY

WHO WAS FRANKLIN?

Rosalind Franklin (1920—1958) was an English chemist who made important discoveries about the structure of DNA. She took the first pictures of DNA, which helped confirm its double-helix shape.

MAKE MARBLE BABIES

Most people agree that the chances of a baby being a male or a female are always the same. This basic concept can be seen in this simple game. How often do you get a female and how often do you get a male?

YOU WILL NEED:

✔ Three marbles of the same color

✔ One similar-sized, different colored marble

✔ Two paper cups

✔ A pen and paper

MOM **DAD**

1 Use the pen to write "MOM" on one of the cups and "DAD" on the other.

2 Place two marbles of the same color in the "MOM" cup. Each of the marbles represents one of a female's two X chromosomes.

3 Place two different colored marbles in the "DAD" cup. This represents the X and Y chromosomes that a male has.

MOM **DAD**

4 Close your eyes and randomly pull one marble out of the "MOM" cup and another from the "DAD" cup to make a marble "baby."

5 Write down the chromosome combination you've made (XX or XY), and note whether this is a male baby or a female baby.

XY

6 Put the marbles back and repeat this experiment at least 20 times. How many males and females did you make?

HOW DOES IT WORK?

You should have gotten a similar number of female and male babies. The odds of a baby being a female (or a male) are almost 50:50. It doesn't matter whether parents have had five females in row, the chances of their next baby being a male is still almost 50%.

ADAPTATION AND EVOLUTION

Life on Earth has been on quite a remarkable journey. Small changes passed from parent to child are responsible for the staggering diversity of life on our planet.

WHAT'S GOING ON?

MUTATIONS

Every living thing on Earth shares a common ancestor —we are all descended from the first life forms that appeared on our planet around 4 billion years ago. You inherited your genetic code from your parents as they did from theirs. But it is never a perfect process. There are always some mistakes—or **mutations**—when a genetic code is copied.

A simplified model of DNA (see p. 20). There is a mistake or "mutation" in the DNA structure.

what's the BIG idea?

NATURAL SELECTION

Sometimes mutations give an animal an advantage over other members of their species—maybe they run faster and can escape predators. This makes them more likely to survive long enough to have babies and pass that advantage on to their own offspring. This is called **natural selection**—good mutations are more likely to be passed on than bad ones. Over many generations, these small changes add up—that's **evolution.**

WHO WAS DARWIN?

Charles Darwin (1809–1882) was a British naturalist (someone who studies living things), whose famous book *On the Origin of Species* shared his ideas about natural selection and evolution.

THE GALAPAGOS FINCHES

Charles Darwin traveled to the Galapagos Islands (off Ecuador) where he discovered that finches on different islands had different shaped beaks. He suggested their beaks must have changed over time to adapt to the food on each particular island.

Large ground finch

Medium ground finch

Small tree finch

Green warbler finch

EVOLUTION IN FRONT OF OUR EYES

Normally, evolution is a slow process because it takes many years for an animal to grow up and reproduce. But bacteria reproduce incredibly rapidly, and scientists have seen them evolving **resistance** to antibiotics (medicines that destroy bacteria) in just ten days (see also p. 72).

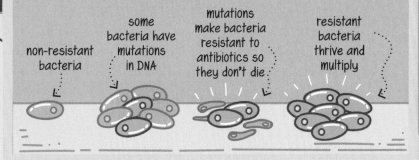

non-resistant bacteria

some bacteria have mutations in DNA

mutations make bacteria resistant to antibiotics so they don't die

resistant bacteria thrive and multiply

WHO WAS LEAKEY?

Mary Leakey (1913–1996) was a British paleoanthropologist (a person who studies the first humans) who found the fossilized skull of an extinct ape, thought to be one of our ancestors.

ADAPTING ANIMALS

Look at the following animals. Can you think of any characteristics that help them thrive in their own particular environment? For instance, a polar bear has evolved white fur, allowing it to camouflage itself against the snow and sneak up on unsuspecting prey. Can you match each animal to a characteristic?

- Humps for fat storage
- Long neck to reach leaves
- Changes color to hide from predators and prey
- Talons and beak to catch prey
- Thick coat for warmth

chameleon

giraffe

eagle

camel

seal

AMAZING ATOMS

Everything in the world is made up of tiny building blocks called atoms. They are so small that, incredibly, a single glass of water contains around 20 million million million million atoms!

WHAT'S GOING ON?

INSIDE AN ATOM

Scientists once thought that an **atom** couldn't be cut up into smaller pieces. But today we know that an atom has two main parts—the nucleus in the middle and **electrons** whizzing around it. Inside the nucleus you'll find two types of particles called **neutrons** and **protons**.

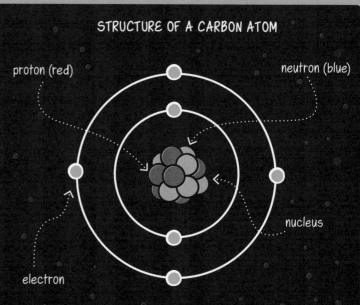

STRUCTURE OF A CARBON ATOM

proton (red)

neutron (blue)

nucleus

electron

what's the BIG idea?

NEUTRAL ATOMS

Protons carry a positive electric **charge**, whereas electrons carry a negative charge. Neutrons have no charge. Inside ordinary atoms, there are the same number of protons and electrons so the charges cancel each other out. If an atom loses or gains electrons, then the overall charge becomes unbalanced and scientists call it an ion.

WHO WAS BOHR?

Niels Bohr (1885–1962) was a Danish physicist who made important discoveries about the way that electrons orbit (circle) the nucleus in atoms.

A SCALE MODEL OF THE ATOM

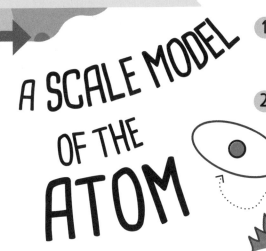

structure of a hydrogen atom

All objects are made of atoms, including this book and the chair you are sitting on. So atoms must be pretty solid objects, right? Let's find out by recreating a scale model of **hydrogen** —the simplest of all types of atoms. Hydrogen has just one proton in the center and one outer electron.

YOU WILL NEED:

✔ An adult helper

✔ A big open space, such as a park

✔ A ball point sewing pin

1 Go to an open space and ask your adult helper to place the pin in the ground.

2 Ask your helper to walk 330 ft (100 m) away from you (roughly 130 steps).

3 If we increased the size of a hydrogen proton to the size of the pin in the ground, then the adult is now the same distance away as the electron. How well can you see him/her? Long way, huh?

330 FEET!

HOW DOES IT WORK?

Atoms are mostly empty space. A hydrogen atom, for example, is 99.9999999999996% empty. Even humans are also mostly empty space. How come, then, you don't fall through a chair when you sit on it? It's all due to something called **electromagnetic force**. The negatively charged electrons in each atom in your bottom and in the chair push against each other and stop you from falling through!

EXTRAORDINARY ELEMENTS

Atoms come in different types called elements. Each element has its own number of protons inside the nucleus. Oxygen, for example, has eight. If it has more or less than eight, then it isn't oxygen!

WHAT'S GOING ON?

THE PERIODIC TABLE

Scientists arrange all the elements they know about into a chart called the Periodic Table of the Elements. Think of it as an ingredients list in a cookbook. Everything around us is made up of these ingredients combined in different ways.

The Periodic Table lists elements that behave in similar ways into groups. Elements appear in the order of their number of protons, starting with hydrogen, which has one, and ending with Oganesson, which has 118!

Groups ·······>

Periods

elements to the right of the black line are non-metals

elements to the left of the black line are metals

1 H Hydrogen																	2 He Helium
3 Li Lithium	4 Be Beryllium											5 B Boron	6 C Carbon	7 N Nitrogen	8 O Oxygen	9 F Fluorine	10 Ne Neon
11 Na Sodium	12 Mg Magnesium											13 Al Aluminum	14 Si Silicon	15 P Phosphorus	16 S Sulfur	17 Cl Chlorine	18 Ar Argon
19 K Potassium	20 Ca Calcium	21 Sc Scandium	22 Ti Titanium	23 V Vanadium	24 Cr Chromium	25 Mn Manganese	26 Fe Iron	27 Co Cobalt	28 Ni Nickel	29 Cu Copper	30 Zn Zinc	31 Ga Gallium	32 Ge Germanium	33 As Arsenic	34 Se Selenium	35 Br Bromine	36 Kr Krypton
37 Rb Rubidium	38 Sr Strontium	39 Y Yttrium	40 Zr Zirconium	41 Nb Niobium	42 Mo Molybdenum	43 Tc Technetium	44 Ru Ruthenium	45 Rh Rhodium	46 Pd Palladium	47 Ag Silver	48 Cd Cadmium	49 In Indium	50 Sn Tin	51 Sb Antimony	52 Te Tellurium	53 I Iodine	54 Xe Xenon
55 Cs Cesium	56 Ba Barium	57-71 Lanthanoids (see below)	72 Hf Hafnium	73 Ta Tantalum	74 W Tungsten	75 Re Rhenium	76 Os Osmium	77 Ir Iridium	78 Pt Platinum	79 Au Gold	80 Hg Mercury	81 Tl Thallium	82 Pb Lead	83 Bi Bismuth	84 Po Polonium	85 At Astatine	86 Rn Radon
87 Fr Francium	88 Ra Radium	89-103 Actinoids (see below)	104 Rf Rutherfordium	105 Db Dubnium	106 Sg Seaborgium	107 Bh Bohrium	108 Hs Hassium	109 Mt Meitnerium	110 Ds Darmstadtium	111 Rg Roentgenium	112 Cn Copernicium	113 Nh Nihonium	114 Fl Flerovium	115 Mc Moscovium	116 Lv Livermorium	117 Ts Tennessine	118 Og Oganesson

57 La Lanthanum	58 Ce Cerium	59 Pr Praseodymium	60 Nd Neodymium	61 Pm Promethium	62 Sm Samarium	63 Eu Europium	64 Gd Gadolinium	65 Tb Terbium	66 Dy Dysprosium	67 Ho Holmium	68 Er Erbium	69 Tm Thulium	70 Yb Ytterbium	71 Lu Lutetium
89 Ac Actinium	90 Th Thorium	91 Pa Protactinium	92 U Uranium	93 Np Neptunium	94 Pu Plutonium	95 Am Americium	96 Cm Curium	97 Bk Berkelium	98 Cf Californium	99 Es Einsteinium	100 Fm Fermium	101 Md Mendelevium	102 No Nobelium	103 Lr Lawrencium

what's the BIG idea?

PERIODS AND GROUPS

The rows across the Periodic Table are called periods. The columns are called groups. Elements in each group behave in similar ways. For example, elements in Group 18 are called Noble gases. They have no smell or color and are very stable. Other elements are more reactive—for instance, cesium explodes when you put it in water!

TRY THIS AT HOME

PERIODIC TABLE DETECTIVE

We go about our daily lives without giving much thought to what the things around us are made of. But the elements of the Periodic Table are everywhere. Let's go on a hunt for them around your home.

1. Take a look at the Periodic Table. Do you recognize any of the names, such as carbon, iron, calcium, and sodium?

2. Collect different household items. Look at the list of ingredients on the back of them or ask an adult what they are made of.

3. Look for the ingredients of each item on the Periodic Table and write them down.

WHO WAS MENDELEEV?

Dmitri Mendeleev (1834–1907) was a Russian chemist who invented an early form of the Periodic Table. The element Mendelevium (number 101) is named after him.

YOU WILL NEED:

✔ A pen and paper

✔ Lots of different household items. For instance: toothpaste, jewelry, food packaging (cereal boxes), soap, drink bottles, shampoo bottles, and so on.

IN FACT...

ARTIFICIAL ELEMENTS

Scientists have been able to create new elements that are not found naturally on the earth. Most of them are named after people or places and include Einsteinium, Nobelium, and Californium.

MOLECULES AND COMPOUNDS

Just like superheroes, atoms and cells can be more powerful when they team up! Scientists, let's find out what happens when atoms join together to become molecules and compounds.

WHAT'S GOING ON?

ORBITING ELECTRONS

The electrons in an atom orbit the nucleus in shells. In the first shell there's space for just two electrons. In outer shells there's room for eight. So an oxygen atom—which has eight electrons—has two in the first shell and six in the second.

STRUCTURE OF AN OXYGEN ATOM

electron in outer shell

neutron (blue)

proton (red)

electron in inner shell

O_2

what's the BIG idea?

MAGNIFICENT MOLECULES

An atom will always try to fill up its shells with electrons. One way it can do this is by sharing electrons with other atoms. Oxygen is missing two electrons in its outer shell. If two atoms of oxygen team up and become a **molecule**, then they can share their electrons and fill the gaps.

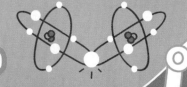

IN FACT...

COVALENT AND IONIC BONDING

There are two ways atoms can bond together to make compounds. Covalent bonding is when they share electrons between them. But there is another way. In ionic bonding, one atom will give up some of its outer electrons to its partner.

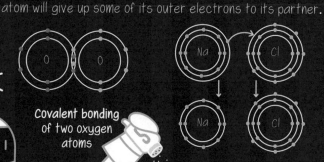

Covalent bonding of two oxygen atoms

Ionic bonding of sodium (left) and chloride (right) atoms to form sodium chloride (salt)

WHO WAS PAULING?

Linus Pauling (1901–1994) was an American chemist who won the Nobel Prize for Chemistry in 1954 for his work on chemical bonds.

IN FACT...

WONDERFUL WATER

Oxygen can find its two missing electrons by bonding with two hydrogen atoms that have one electron each. This makes a molecule called H_2O—or water. A molecule made from two or more elements is called a compound.

TRY THIS AT HOME

MAKE MARSHMALLOW MOLECULES

Some of the most common substances are not elements, but compounds—materials made up of at least two types of atoms joined together. Here you can use marshmallows instead of atoms to create some compounds of your own!

YOU WILL NEED:

- ✔ A bag of marshmallows of different colors
- ✔ Some wooden skewers

1 This is what the structure of water—H_2O—would look like if we made it out of marshmallows.

hydrogen

hydrogen

oxygen

2 Can you make a model of the following compounds in the same way?

AMMONIA (NH_3—one atom of nitrogen and three atoms of hydrogen)
METHANE (CH_4—one atom of carbon and four atoms of hydrogen)
CARBON DIOXIDE (CO_2—one atom of carbon and two atoms of oxygen)

IN FACT...

SNOWFLAKES

Snowflakes are crystals made of trillions of water molecules. They don't all look the same under a microscope. That's because when they fall to the ground they don't all pass through exactly the same air temperature or moisture, so they form slightly differently.

MIX IT UP!

Good scientists know that there are different ways to combine materials together. Atoms can be chemically bonded to each other to make molecules, but you can also create mixtures of different materials.

WHAT'S GOING ON?

DISSOLVING

One of the easiest ways to create a mixture is by dissolving something into a liquid. For example, you can dissolve salt into water. The liquid is called the solvent, and the thing being dissolved is called the solute. The mixture of the two is called a solution.

solute

SOLVENT

SOLUTION

IN FACT...

TEMPERATURE MATTERS

A solute will dissolve more quickly if the solvent is heated. A higher temperature produces more energy and the solvent's molecules move around faster. This means they bump into molecules of the solute more often, and so the solute dissolves faster.

TEMPERATURE INCREASES ·······>

WHO WAS HENRY?

William Henry (1774–1836) was an English chemist famous for his work on dissolving gases into liquids.

what's the BIG idea?

RECYCLING

We are all told to recycle as much as we can because it's better for the environment. But have you ever thought about how your mixed up recyclables are sorted? Iron and steel are magnetic, while aluminum isn't—so recycling centers use huge magnets to separate these metals from each other.

SEPARATING SALT AND SAND

Some mixtures are easy to separate, but others take a lot of effort. In this experiment you're going to learn how to separate a mixture of salt and sand.

YOU WILL NEED:

✔ An adult helper
✔ A tablespoon of salt
✔ A tablespoon of sand
✔ 3 1/2 fl oz (100 ml) of water
✔ A fine mesh strainer
✔ Two cups
✔ A pot
✔ A stove or hot plate
✔ A small spoon

WARNING! HOT POT

1 First, add the salt and the sand to one of the cups, and stir well to create a mixture.

2 Add the water to the same cup and stir until the salt dissolves (but the sand won't).

3 Pass the salty, sandy water through the strainer into the second cup.

4 The sand won't pass through, so you'll be left with just salty water in the cup.

5 Add the salty water to the pot and ask an adult to heat it on a stove or hot plate until the water evaporates. You'll be left with the salt at the bottom of the pot.

ACIDS AND BASES

Have you ever accidentally squirted lemon juice in your eye? It hurts, right? That's because it's an acid. The opposite of an acid is a base.

WHAT'S GOING ON?

DOWN TO HYDROGEN

Whether a chemical is an **acid** or a **base** depends on its chemical structure. Acids have lots of hydrogen ions in them. These are hydrogen atoms that have lost their only electron, and so they have a positive electrical charge. Bases have many hydroxide ions (hydrogen stuck to oxygen).

what's the BIG idea?

pH SCALE

Scientists have a way of measuring how acidic or basic a substance is. It is called the pH scale and it runs from 0–14. Water is neutral and has a pH of 7. Low pH numbers are acidic and high pH numbers are basic.

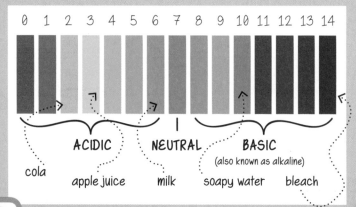

0 1 2 3 4 5 6 7 8 9 10 11 12 13 14

ACIDIC — NEUTRAL — BASIC (also known as alkaline)

cola — apple juice — milk — soapy water — bleach

IN FACT...

STOMACH ACID

Your stomach is full of an acid called hydrochloric acid, which measures 2 or 3 on the pH scale. It helps digest the food you eat.

WHO WAS SØRENSEN?

S.P.L. Sørensen (1868–1939) was a Danish chemist who came up with the idea of the pH scale.

MAKE YOUR OWN pH INDICATOR

You don't always need special chemicals to perform scientific experiments. In this activity you'll make a liquid that will help you find out if something is an acid or a base. Ask an adult to help you!

YOU WILL NEED:

- ✔ An adult helper
- ✔ A head of red cabbage
- ✔ A bowl
- ✔ A kettle
- ✔ A knife
- ✔ A strainer
- ✔ Three clear cups
- ✔ Water
- ✔ Liquid bleach
- ✔ White vinegar

WARNING! SHARP KNIFE, HOT WATER, AND BLEACH!

1 Fill the kettle with water, and boil it. Ask an adult for help.

2 With adult help, cut the red cabbage into small pieces. You'll only need about half of it.

3 Add the cabbage pieces to the bowl, and ask an adult to fill it up with boiling water.

4 Leave it to cool.

5 Drain the purple water through a strainer to remove the cabbage.

6 You now have your pH indicator.

7 Half fill the three plastic cups with the bleach, vinegar, and plain water.

8 Pour some of your pH indicator into each cup. What happens?

HOW DOES IT WORK?

Red cabbage contains compounds called anthocyanins that change color in the presence of acids and bases. It goes green-yellow with bases (the bleach), stays purple with neutral substances (the water), and goes reddish pink when it comes in contact with acids (the vinegar).

BLEACH   VINEGAR   WATER

CHEMICAL REACTIONS

Chemical reactions occur all around us all the time. Some you'll barely notice, but others can give spectacular results. Let's investigate!

➡ what's the **BIG** idea?

INTERACTING BONDS

A **chemical reaction** happens when at least two molecules or atoms interact with each other. Bonds are broken, and new bonds are made. Rusting metal is a good example. Oxygen in the air combines with iron (in the presence of water) to create iron oxide (the scientific name for rust), which changes the structure of the metal in the reaction.

TRY THIS AT HOME

MAKE ELEPHANT TOOTHPASTE

Some chemical reactions can be quite dramatic! Let's make a crazy substance that looks a lot like something an elephant might use as toothpaste! Make sure you have adult supervision.

YOU WILL NEED:

- ✔ An adult helper
- ✔ A 33 fl oz (1 liter) plastic bottle
- ✔ Rubber gloves
- ✔ A funnel
- ✔ 3 1/2 fl oz (100 ml) of 40 Volume Hydrogen Peroxide
- ✔ Dishwashing liquid
- ✔ Food coloring
- ✔ 1/4 oz (7 g) packet of dried yeast
- ✔ A cup
- ✔ 4 tablespoons of warm water
- ✔ Plastic wrap

1. Use the plastic wrap to cover your work area. This is going to get messy!

2. Put on the rubber gloves, and use the funnel to pour the hydrogen peroxide into the bottle.

3. Add a drop of the dishwashing liquid and the food coloring, and swirl around to mix.

4. Mix the yeast and the warm water together in the cup.

5. Add the contents of the cup to the bottle, and watch what happens!

WARNING: MESSY! PEROXIDE CAN BURN!

WHO WAS BERTHOLLET?

Claude Louis Berthollet (1748–1822) was a French chemist who was the first to realize that some chemical reactions are reversible—in other words, you can undo them.

TRY THIS AT HOME

THE NAKED EGG

Follow these steps, and you'll be able to watch a chemical reaction unfold before your very eyes as you make the shell of an egg disappear!

YOU WILL NEED:

✔ A glass or plastic jar with a lid (must be see through)

✔ 33 fl oz (1 liter) of white vinegar

✔ A raw egg

1. Add 16 fl oz (500 ml) of vinegar to the jar, and carefully drop in the egg.

2. Put on the lid and leave it for 24 hours.

3. Carefully drain off the vinegar and replace it with another 16 fl oz (500 ml) of vinegar.

4. Check back regularly over the next few days to see what you notice if you look closely at the egg.

HOW DOES IT WORK?

Vinegar contains acetic acid. The egg shell is made of calcium carbonate. A chemical reaction strips the egg shell away, creating calcium acetate, as well as water and carbon dioxide (CO_2). You can see the CO_2 as tiny bubbles clinging to the egg.

35

SOLIDS, LIQUIDS, AND GASES

In the world around us, materials exist in three main states of matter. They can be either solids, liquids, or gases. Scientists, let's take a look!

→ what's the **BIG** idea?

CHANGING STATES

You can change the state of a substance by heating or cooling it, because this increases or decreases the energy of its particles. There are four main processes by which matter can change state: **melting**, **freezing**, **condensation**, and **evaporation**.

GAS

SUBLIMATION — heating

DEPOSITION — cooling

EVAPORATION — heating

CONDENSATION — cooling

MELTING — heating

FREEZING — cooling

SOLID   LIQUID

WHAT'S GOING ON?

ALL IN THE PARTICLES

All **matter** is made of particles: atoms or molecules. Solids, liquids, and gases behave in different ways because of the way their particles are arranged. In solids, the particles are held together in a rigid structure and cannot move around. That's why solids keep their shapes. In liquids, the particles are still attracted to each other, but are able to move around. That's why you can pour liquids. In gases, the particles are free to fly around at high speed, which is why they are easy to compress but need to be contained within a lid!

IN FACT...

SKIPPING STAGES

Under special conditions, a solid can skip the liquid phase and turn straight into a gas. This is called sublimation. Going directly from a gas to a solid is called **deposition**.

SOLID   LIQUID   GAS

BOILING POINTS

Water boils at 212°F (100°C) at sea level. However, at the top of mountains, such as Mt. Everest at 29,029 ft (8,848 m), the pressure of air is much lower, so water boils (and turns to gas) at just 158°F (70°C).

TRY THIS AT HOME

THE ICE LIFTER

Do you think it is possible to lift an ice cube out of some water without ever touching it? Use this clever trick to impress your friends with your magic skills!

YOU WILL NEED:

- ✔ A bowl of water
- ✔ An ice cube
- ✔ String
- ✔ Salt

1. Place the ice cube in the water so it floats.

2. Place one end of the string on top of the ice cube.

3. Sprinkle some salt over the same end of the string.

4. Leave it for one minute.

5. Pull on the other end of the string to lift the ice cube out of the water.

HOW DOES IT WORK?

Adding the salt forces the ice cube to melt slightly. When the water refreezes, it also freezes the string in place. This is why we add salt to icy roads to make them less slippery—it makes ice melt.

WHO WAS VAN DER WAALS?

Johannes van der Waals (1837–1923) was a Dutch physicist who is famous for working out the forces between molecules in liquids and gases.

GRAVITY

In our everyday lives, a force called gravity is always pulling us downward. If you jump, you can defy this force for a very short time. But if you want to beat gravity for longer, then you need powerful machines, such as planes and rockets.

what's the BIG idea?

A FALLING APPLE

Have you heard the story about the English physicist Sir Isaac Newton (1643–1727) and his discovery of **gravity**? He was sitting under a tree when an apple fell on his head. In that moment he realized there must be a force pulling it down, and that same force attracted the moon to the earth and the earth to the sun.

IN FACT...

GRAVITY ON OTHER PLANETS

The strength of gravity depends on the mass of a planet or moon. (The mass is the amount of matter that makes up an object). For a small object, such as the moon, gravity is weaker than on Earth. But on a big planet like Jupiter, that has 317.8 times the mass of Earth, gravity is much stronger.

Jupiter

Earth

FALLING OBJECTS

Objects fall to the ground because the gravity of the earth pulls them down. But does gravity affect all things in the same way? Grab some everyday items and investigate for yourself!

YOU WILL NEED:

✔ A large ball, such as a soccer ball, volleyball, or basketball

✔ A small ball, such as a tennis ball or golf ball

✔ A piece of paper

✔ A staircase

1 Take the big ball and the small ball and stand at the top of the staircase. Before you drop the balls, make a prediction as to which one will hit the ground first.

2 Now, drop the balls from the same height to see if you made the correct prediction.

3 Take one of the balls and the sheet of paper. Will the paper or the ball hit the ground first?

4 Drop the ball and the paper to find out.

HOW DOES IT WORK?

Around 1590, the Italian scientist Galileo Galilei (see p. 63) realized that objects of different masses fall to the ground at the same rate. But what about your experiment with the paper? It took longer because it was slowed down by the air.

In 1971, U.S. astronaut Dave Scott dropped a hammer and a feather on the moon (where there is no air). Both objects hit the lunar surface at the same time.

SPARKS AND VOLTS

In the modern world we are never far from electricity, from the lights in our homes to the chargers for our phones and tablets. It's all possible thanks to the movement of the tiny particles we call electrons!

WHAT'S GOING ON?

FREE FLOWING ELECTRONS

Electrons are normally stuck to the nucleus of atoms (see p. 24). However, in some materials they come loose and move from one atom to another. This flow of "free" electrons is what creates electric current.

one electron moves to the next atom

one electron moves to the next atom

and so on...

electrons

nucleus—protons and neutrons

FLOW OF ELECTRICITY

what's the BIG idea?

ELECTRICAL CIRCUITS

The **electricity** in our homes is based on the idea of an electrical circuit—a complete path that allows electricity to flow all the way around. If you break the circuit, the electricity cannot flow. A simple electric circuit carries electric charge from the negative end of a battery around the wires and back to the positive end.

light bulb

wires

negative end

A SIMPLE CIRCUIT

battery

positive end

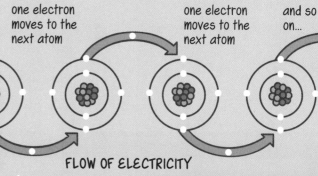

WHO WAS VOLTA?

Alessandro Volta (1745–1827) was an Italian scientist who built the first electric battery. The volt, a unit to measure electricity, is named after him.

what's the BIG idea?

CONDUCTORS AND INSULATORS

Some materials allow electrons to move easily through them. We call these conductors, and they include copper, aluminum, and steel. Materials that don't conduct electricity, such as wood and plastic, are called insulators.

WHO WAS TESLA?

Nikola Tesla (1856–1943) was a Serbian-American physicist and inventor who helped develop the electrical current systems that run into our homes today.

IN FACT...
LIGHTNING

Lightning is nature's spectacular display of fierce electricity. During a thunderstorm, negatively charged electrons collect at the bottom of a cloud and search for the quickest route to a positive charge—which is often found on the ground. We see this as a bolt of lightning.

TRY THIS AT HOME

BENDING WATER

Impress your friends by performing this experiment where you can bend water and act like a powerful magician!

1 Turn on the faucet so that a slow and steady stream of water flows out of it.

2 Take the comb and comb your hair with it at least ten times (always in the same direction).

3 Bring the comb close to the stream of water. What happens?

4 Act like a true scientist and investigate further. Does hot or cold water make a difference? What about the distance between the water and the comb? What else can you discover?

YOU WILL NEED:

✔ A sink with a faucet
✔ A plastic comb
✔ Clean hair

HOW DOES IT WORK?

By combing your hair, you build up electrons on the comb that give it an overall negative charge. Those negative charges attract the positive charges in the water toward them, bending the water stream toward the comb.

MAGNET MAGIC

Playing with magnets is incredibly fun. They can attract and move objects made of iron or steel as if by magic. But it isn't really magic—there is a force at work called the electromagnetic force.

what's the BIG idea?

OPPOSITES ATTRACT

A simple magnet has two poles—north and south. When you bring two poles that are the same together, the electromagnetic force pushes them apart—they repel. But two opposite poles attract each other and the two magnets stick together.

WHAT'S GOING ON?

MAGNETIC FIELD

All objects that exert a force have an area around them where the force acts. Physicists call this area a field. The area around a magnet is called the magnetic field.

IN FACT...

THE EARTH IS A MAGNET

The core of Earth is made from liquid iron and nickel. As Earth turns, this liquid moves and generates a magnetic field around our planet. The magnetic field acts as a shield, protecting life on Earth from dangerous energy from space.

WHO WAS MAXWELL?

James Clerk Maxwell (1831–1879) was a Scottish physicist who showed that electricity and magnetism are closely related to one another.

TRUE NORTH OR MAGNETIC NORTH?

True north is the direction along the earth's surface to the North Pole. Magnetic north is the direction of the earth's magnetic field lines to the Magnetic North Pole, which is found at a slight angle to the North Pole.

READ A COMPASS

A compass has a magnetized needle that spins toward Earth's Magnetic North. If you want to find Magnetic North, you gently turn the compass so that it's needle lines up with "N."

TRY THIS AT HOME

MAKE YOUR OWN COMPASS

You can't see it, but the earth's magnetic field is all around us. A compass uses our planet's magnetism to help you find your way. But you don't need to buy an expensive compass—you can make your own out of everyday items!

YOU WILL NEED:

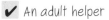

✔ An adult helper
✔ A plastic bottle cap
✔ A sewing needle
✔ A bar magnet
✔ A small dish filled with water

WARNING! NEEDLE!

1 Float the bottle cap upside down in the water.

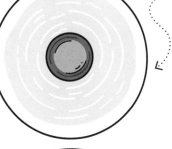

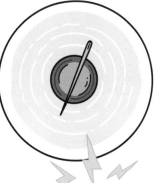

50 TIMES!

2 Stroke the needle with the magnet 50 times from bottom to top (pointed end to eye) with the same pole of the magnet.

3 Carefully place the needle on top of the bottle cap.

4 What happens?

5 Slowly bring the bar magnet closer to the needle. What happens now? Which is stronger: the magnetic field of the magnet or Earth's?

HOW DOES IT WORK?

Inside the steel needle are thousands of regions called domains. Stroking them with the magnet causes the domains to line up the same way, so the needle becomes magnetic. It then swivels to line up with Earth's magnetic field so that the needle faces Magnetic North along a North/South line. When you hold your magnet next to the needle, the needle moves. Even a small bar magnet is much stronger than Earth's magnetic field.

TRICK OF THE LIGHT

Without light we wouldn't be able to see anything around us. Light is also why our world is full of beautiful, vivid colors from the blue of the sky to the green of a tree to the pink of strawberry ice cream!

what's the BIG idea?

COLOR

You might think light is white or has no color. The sun's light is actually made up of seven different colors. If light is split by a prism or even a drop of water, its colors form a spectrum—the colors of the rainbow. We see things because light bounces off them. Most objects don't give off light—it's the light reflecting off them that you see. A white object reflects all colors and a black object absorbs all colors.

white

red
orange
yellow
green
blue
indigo
violet

TRY THIS AT HOME

A BENDY PENCIL

In this optical illusion you can make it seem as if a pencil is broken when it isn't!

YOU WILL NEED:

✔ A glass of water
✔ A pencil

1 Fill up the glass with water until it is nearly full.

2 Drop the pencil into the water.

3 Look at the pencil through the side of the glass. Look at where the top of the water meets the air. Does the pencil look straight?

STRAIGHT LINES

Light always travels in straight lines. However, the direction in which light travels can be changed. Light can be bent or **refracted** when it passes between two substances that have different densities (compactness), such as air and water. The pencil in your glass looks broken at the point where light emerges from the water and enters into the air.

TRY THIS AT HOME

CREATE A RAINBOW

You don't have to wait for rain to see a rainbow. You can make your own! Just follow these instructions.

YOU WILL NEED:

✔ A shallow tray such as a baking tray

✔ Water

✔ A small mirror

✔ Some white paper

1 Take the tray to a sunny spot.

2 Pour water into the tray until it is half full.

3 Lay the mirror against one end of the tray so it is half in and half out of the water.

4 Position the tray so that the sun shines on the submerged part of the mirror.

5 Hold the paper above the tray, over the mirror.

6 With a little adjustment, you'll see a rainbow projected onto the underside of the paper.

HOW DOES IT WORK?

SPLITTING LIGHT

As sunlight passes through the water, the water splits the white light into its many colors, just as raindrops do when they pass through a rainbow.

SOUNDS GREAT!

Each day we hear a huge variety of sounds, including birds singing, car engines humming, and people laughing. These sounds are all tiny vibrations in the air around us.

WHAT'S GOING ON?

LISTEN UP!

When we hear a friend speak there is a lot of complex stuff going on. First, vibrating folds of skin inside his or her larynx (voice box) vibrate the air around them. The vibrations pass through the air in all directions, and some of the vibrations will reach your ear and make your eardrums vibrate. The vibrations pass to three small bones and to the cochlea in your inner ear. Then a nerve picks up these signals and passes them to the brain, which interprets the signals as sound.

outer ear

eardrum

small bones

ear lobe

cochlea

what's the BIG idea?

SOUND WAVES

Sound travels in waves. Frequency is a measure of how often a wave repeats. Lots of waves in a short period of time (high frequency) create a high-**pitched** sound. We hear longer waves as a low-pitched sound. Amplitude is how much energy a sound has. The greater the energy, the bigger the peaks in the waves and the louder the sound. Sound waves don't just travel through air—they can also travel through liquids and solids.

LOW FREQUENCY
Longer waves = lower pitch

HIGH FREQUENCY
Shorter waves = higher pitch

quieter

louder

LOW AMPLITUDE (ENERGY)
Low peaks = quieter

HIGH AMPLITUDE (ENERGY)
High peaks = louder

PLAY YOUR OWN MUSICAL INSTRUMENT

Musical instruments, such as guitars, can create lots of different sounds because you can vibrate their strings in lots of ways. By following these instructions you can make your own musical instrument! See what kind of music you can play.

YOU WILL NEED:

- ✔ Four identical clear glass bottles
- ✔ Water
- ✔ A measuring cup
- ✔ Food coloring (optional)
- ✔ Keyboard or piano (optional)

1 First you need to know how much water each bottle can hold. If it isn't written on the bottle, fill up one bottle and pour it out into the measuring cup to find out.

2 Leave one bottle empty, then fill the others up so they are a quarter full, half full, and three-quarters full.

3 You can add different food coloring to each bottle at this stage if you want to make your musical instrument colorful.

4 Blow across the top of each bottle and listen carefully to the sounds created. Does more water create a higher or a lower pitched sound?

5 If you have access to a keyboard or piano, try to find the key (musical note) that matches each bottle. How far apart are they on the keyboard?

HOW DOES IT WORK?

Air vibrating in a small space (so in the most full bottle) will have the highest pitched sound. A bottle with twice as much water creates a sound with twice the frequency. That means they are one octave (or eight white keys) apart on a keyboard.

LET'S GET MOVING!

We use energy all the time, whether for running at the playground or for plugging our tablets in to charge. Energy is the ability to do something.

what's the BIG idea?

CONVERSION OF ENERGY

Energy cannot be created or destroyed. It can only be changed—or converted—from one form to another. In a light bulb, for example, electrical energy is converted into heat energy and light energy.

RENEWABLE OR NON-RENEWABLE ENERGY?

We get our energy from many different places. Some comes from fossil fuels (fuels made from the remains of living things in the ground) such as coal, oil, and natural gas. These are non-renewables —when they run out they are gone. Energy sources that are renewable include solar (from the sun), wind, and wave power.

NON-RENEWABLE

RENEWABLE

CAR RAMPS

Now you're going to learn about the relationship between two types of energy —**potential** and **kinetic**—by rolling toy cars down a slope.

1 On the paper, draw a table with two columns. Write "Books" at the top of the first column and "Distance" at the top of the other.

2 Rest the plank of wood on the edge of one book to create a ramp.

3 Hold the car at the top of the ramp and let it go (don't push it).

4 Use the tape measure to see how far from the bottom of the ramp the car traveled. Write your answer in your table.

5 What do you think will happen if you use more books? Write down your prediction.

6 Repeat the experiment with two, three, four, and five books, and write your findings in the table.

YOU WILL NEED:

- ✔ Five books of roughly the same thickness
- ✔ A plank of wood
- ✔ A toy car
- ✔ A tape measure
- ✔ A pen and paper

HOW DOES IT WORK?

The higher the car starts, the more potential (stored) energy it has. This is converted into a type of movement energy called kinetic energy as the car moves down the slope. Greater kinetic energy means the car picks up greater speed and travels farther from the end of the ramp.

WHO WAS JOULE?

James Joule (1818–1889) was an English physicist who made important discoveries about energy. The unit of measure, the joule (J), is named after him.

IN FACT...

ENERGY AND JOULES

Energy is measured in joules. Joules measure the amount of energy transferred (also called work done) when you apply force on an object. One joule of work is completed when a force of 1 N (or Newton) is applied over a distance of 3.28 ft (1 meter). A person sprinting uses about 1,000 joules per second.

HEAT AND TEMPERATURE

We are used to dealing with heat and temperature all the time, whether we're talking about the weather, boiling water, or freezing food. But what exactly is it, scientists?

what's the BIG idea?

ENERGY LEVELS

When you heat something you give the molecules in that substance extra energy, so they move around faster. When you cool something you remove energy, and the atoms slow down.

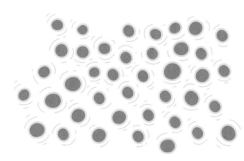

particles in
something cold

particles in
something hot

IN FACT...

HEAT OR TEMPERATURE?

Heat and temperature are not the same thing. Heat (measured in Joules) is the total amount of energy of all the molecules in a substance. Temperature (measured in degrees) is the average energy of a molecule.

A thermometer measures temperature in Fahrenheit (F) or Celsius (C). ---->

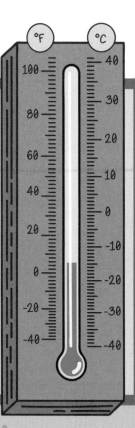

WHO WAS CELSIUS?

Anders Celsius (1701–1744) was a Swedish scientist who experimented with temperature. The Celsius (°C) temperature scale is named after him. The Fahrenheit (°F) scale is named after the Polish physicist Daniel Fahrenheit (1686–1736).

HEAT FLOW IN ACTION

In this incredible experiment you are going to see for yourself how temperature affects the **density** (compactness) of materials. It gets wet, so you may want to do this in a sink!

cold water   hot water

1 First, fill one of the jars to the brim with cold water and fill another jar to the brim with hot water.

2 Add the blue food coloring to the cold water, and stir it with the spoon. Do the same with the red food coloring and the hot water.

3 Stand the blue jar inside the tray. Then put the acetate sheet on top and press down.

4 You should now be able to turn the blue jar upside down without any water spilling out.

YOU WILL NEED:

✔ An adult helper
✔ A tray
✔ Four glass jars
✔ Red and blue food coloring
✔ Two acetate sheets
✔ Cold water
✔ Hot water
✔ A spoon

cold water

WARNING! VERY WET!

5 Put the red jar into the tray, and then place the blue jar upside down on top of it so that the edges of the jars line up.

6 Ask an adult to hold the top of the blue jar while you carefully pull out the acetate sheet from between the jars. What happens?

cold water

hot water

7 Make another red and another blue jar using the remaining two jars. Repeat the steps above, but place the red jar on top of the blue jar this time.

8 Now what happens when you pull out the acetate sheet?

HOW DOES IT WORK?

Cold water is denser (more compact) than hot water because its molecules are closer together. In the first experiment, the denser cold water sank into the hot water and the two liquids mixed. But, in the second experiment, the heavier liquid was already at the bottom, so the liquids did not mix.

hot water

cold and hot water mix

cold water

ROCKS AND FOSSILS

Rocks are some of the oldest things around us. Many have been lying unchanged for billions of years! Hidden in some of them are fossils that tell us about the history of life on Earth.

what's the BIG idea?

TYPES OF ROCK

There are three main types of rock: igneous, sedimentary, and metamorphic. Igneous rocks are formed when magma (very hot liquid rock under the earth's surface) cools. Sedimentary rocks are created when layers of sand, clay, and the bones of dead animals are crushed together over millions of years. Metamorphic rocks are those that have been changed by heat or pressure.

TRY THIS AT HOME

BE A GEOLOGIST

Have you ever wondered what rocks are made of? Start a rock collection and perform the "acid test" used by geologists (scientists who study what the earth is made of) to find out what your rock is made of.

1. Set out your plastic cups—one for each rock you want to test.

2. Pour the same amount of vinegar into each cup.

3. Place a small rock into each cup.

4. Do any of them start to fizz? Do some fizz more than others?

YOU WILL NEED:

- ✔ Various small rock samples that you've collected
- ✔ Plastic cups
- ✔ Vinegar

HOW DOES IT WORK?

If a rock contains calcium carbonate then it will react with the vinegar to produce carbon dioxide, which will create bubbles, or fizzing. The more a rock fizzes the more calcium carbonate is present.

IN FACT...

HOW OLD IS EARTH?

Our planet must be at least as old as its oldest rocks. The oldest rocks found by geologists are more than 4 billion years old. Scientists have calculated that Earth is 4.54 billion years old.

WHO WAS LYELL?

Charles Lyell (1797–1875) was a British geologist who was one of the first scientists to use rocks to argue that Earth is much older than people had once suspected.

what's the BIG idea?

FOSSILS

When a plant or animal dies, its body can become trapped inside sand or mud. As more layers are added over millions of years to form sedimentary rock, an imprint of its body forms in the rock. Scientists call these imprints fossils.

IN FACT...

EGGS-TRA

It isn't just body parts that can be preserved as fossils. Paleontologists—scientists who study fossils—have also found fossilized footprints and eggs.

WHO WAS ANNING?

Mary Anning (1799–1847) was a British paleontologist who found important fossils on England's coastline. She identified the first ichthyosaur and plesiosaur dinosaurs.

VOLCANOES AND EARTHQUAKES

Nature can be beautiful, but it can also be incredibly violent. Volcanoes and earthquakes show the natural world at its most ferocious.

what's the BIG idea?

TECTONIC PLATES

The earth's surface is not one complete surface—like a jigsaw puzzle, it is made up of smaller, interlocking pieces called tectonic plates. These plates float on an ocean of hot, liquid rock called magma, so the plates move around.

North American plate

Eurasian plate

Arabian plate

Pacific plate

African plate

Indo-Australian plate

Nazca plate

South American plate

Antarctic plate

WHAT'S GOING ON?

NATURE'S FORCES

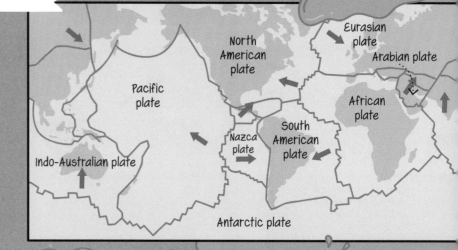

VOLCANO

EARTHQUAKE

A border between tectonic plates is called a boundary. Sometimes the movement of the plates causes cracks at these boundaries known as faults. Earthquakes occur when two plates rub against each other at one of these faults. If two tectonic plates meet, one can be forced underneath the other. This process forces magma upward where it can burst out of the earth's surface. As it cools down, it turns into solid rock and forms a volcano.

CONTINENTAL DRIFT

Have you ever noticed how South America and Africa fit together like puzzle pieces? Some 300 million years ago, all the world's continents were joined in a large landmass called Pangaea. But the continents drifted apart over many millions of years, floating on an ocean of magma.

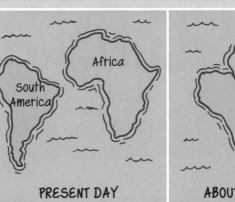

PRESENT DAY

ABOUT 300 MILLION YEARS AGO

TRY THIS AT HOME

MAKE YOUR OWN VOLCANO

In this fun, messy experiment you can recreate the wonder of a volcanic eruption from the safety of your own home!

YOU WILL NEED:

✔ An adult helper
✔ Vinegar
✔ Baking soda
✔ Red food coloring
✔ Dishwashing liquid
✔ A teaspoon
✔ A small container, such as a baby food jar
✔ Papier mâché or modeling clay

WARNING! MESSY!

1. Your first job is to build the volcano itself. You can do this using papier mâché or modeling clay. You need a hollow space in the center for the lava to erupt from.

2. Add two teaspoons of baking soda and one teaspoon of dishwashing liquid to the small container.

3. Add a few drops of the red food coloring to the container.

4. Take your volcano outside, and place the container inside of it.

5. Measure five teaspoons of vinegar, and add it to the container.

6. Watch as your volcano suddenly and spectacularly erupts!

HOW DOES IT WORK?

Vinegar is an acid and baking soda is a base (see p. 32). When they meet, they create a chemical reaction that quickly releases lots of the gas carbon dioxide. This becomes trapped in the bubbles of dishwashing liquid.

THE OCEANS

Look at the earth from space and the most obvious thing about it is that it's very blue. That's because 71% of the planet's surface is covered in water.

➡ what's the **BIG** idea?

FIVE OCEANS

The earth has five main oceans: The Atlantic, The Arctic, The Indian, The Pacific, and The Southern oceans.

IN FACT...

SALTY WATER

The salt in seawater comes from rocks on land. Raindrops wear away the rock and carry some of its salt out to sea.

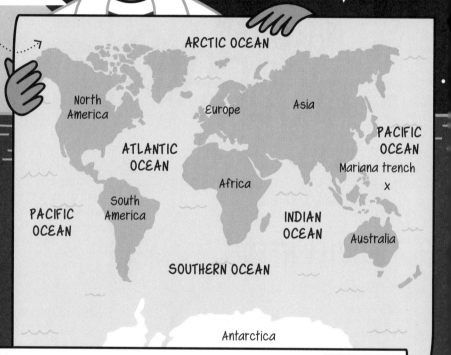

ARCTIC OCEAN

North America

Europe

Asia

PACIFIC OCEAN

Mariana trench
x

ATLANTIC OCEAN

Africa

PACIFIC OCEAN

South America

INDIAN OCEAN

Australia

SOUTHERN OCEAN

Antarctica

IN FACT...

THE MARIANA TRENCH

This trench is the deepest point in the world's oceans, located in the Pacific Ocean. At nearly 36,090 ft (11,000 m) deep, if you placed Mt. Everest in the trench its peak would still be underwater!

DEPTH IN FEET

0
6,561
13,123
19,685
26,246
32,808
36,089

Mariana Trench

Mt. Everest 29,029 ft (8,848 m) high

Bottom of trench, 36,070 ft (10,994 m) deep

what's the BIG idea?

TIDES

Have you ever been at the seaside and seen the water creep up the sand or flow away from the beach? These **tides** are caused by the gravitational pull of the moon (and sun) on Earth's water. Most coasts have two high tides and two low tides each day.

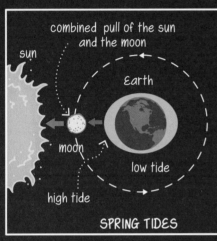

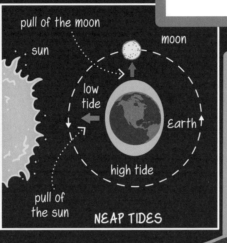

TRY THIS AT HOME

BUILD A TIDE POOL

Tide pools are rocky pools on the seashore. Some are pools only during a low tide but are fully covered by the sea during high tide. The pools are home to sealife that have to cope with tides and waves.

YOU WILL NEED:

- ✔ A big tray or tin with sides about 2½ in (6 cm) high
- ✔ Sand
- ✔ Different-sized rocks and stones
- ✔ Plastic sea creatures and plants, such as starfish, fish, sea urchins, crabs, seaweed, sea anemone, clams, limpets, etc. (or you can make these out of modeling clay).

1 Lay a 1-cm thick layer of sand at the bottom of the tray.

2 Add some stones and rocks to the tray. Pile some of them up in one corner. Arrange them at different levels to create a tide pool.

3 Place the sea creatures in different places in the pool.

4 Gradually add some water and see which animals are submerged first. Why not make some waves in your tide pool, and watch what happens.

HOW DOES IT WORK?

A small amount of water in your pool represents a low tide, and a lot of water represents a high tide. Think about which animals are always covered with water and which animals are sometimes in air and sometimes in water depending on the tides.

WATER, WATER EVERYWHERE!

When pouring yourself a drink of water, have you ever stopped to think where that water comes from? Its journey to your glass is incredible!

WHAT'S GOING ON?

EVAPORATION AND CONDENSATION

Most of the world's water is in the oceans. As the water is warmed by the air, some of it evaporates and rises into the air in gas form called water vapor. The higher it gets, the cooler it gets. Eventually, this vapor turns back into water droplets or even ice crystals that gather—or **condense**—around tiny particles of dust in the sky to form clouds.

condensation

precipitation

evaporation

ground water

IN FACT...

DID YOU KNOW?

Water stays in the ocean for an average of 3,200 years.

what's the BIG idea?

PRECIPITATION

If too many water droplets or ice crystals gather together, a cloud can no longer hold them and they fall down to the ground as raindrops or snowflakes. This is called precipitation. The largest raindrops fall at 20 miles an hour, and raindrops can take between 2 and 7 minutes to hit the ground.

RESERVOIRS

Reservoirs are huge, human-made, open-air water tanks that collect rain. The water is then filtered and cleaned before being sent along underground pipes to your home.

IN FACT...

THE SMELL OF RAIN

Has your nose ever told you that it's about to rain? Rain has a very distinctive, pleasant smell that scientists call petrichor. It is strongest when it first rains after a long period of warm, dry weather. The raindrops hit the ground and release distinctive smelling chemicals from the soil.

TRY THIS AT HOME

RAIN IN A GLASS

You don't have to wait for clouds to gather to see rain. You can make it rain in your own home in this simple experiment.

YOU WILL NEED:

✔ A glass
✔ Shaving cream
✔ Blue food coloring
✔ A pipette

1 Fill the glass most of the way up with water from the faucet.

2 Squirt some shaving cream on top of the glass to create your own cloud.

3 Slowly drip drops of food coloring onto the shaving cream using the pipette.

4 Keep an eye on the water underneath.

HOW DOES IT WORK?

When you first add the food coloring, not much happens. But as droplets of food coloring gather together, they become too heavy for the shaving cream to support and they drop down into the water below. This is similar to how water collects in a cloud before tumbling out as rain.

WEATHER WATCH

The weather affects us everyday. It governs the clothes we choose to wear, how we decide to travel, and can even change our mood.

WHAT'S GOING ON?

WEATHER OR CLIMATE?

Although many people use these words to mean the same thing, weather and **climate** are different. Weather is what the conditions outside are like from day-to-day. Climate is how the weather behaves over a long period of time.

LOCATION	CLIMATE	WEATHER
Kuala Lumpur, Malaysia	Tropical	86°F (30°C) Hot with rain showers
Paris, France	Temperate	62°F (17°C) Mild with some sunny spells
Cairo, Egypt	Desert	110°F (44°C) Hot and dry

carbon dioxide gas from burning fossil fuels

HEAT FROM SUN

heat trapped by carbon dioxide gas in atmosphere

heat from sea

heat from land

carbon dioxide gas from car exhaust

what's the BIG idea?

CLIMATE CHANGE

The earth's climate is constantly changing. In the past it's been through periods called **ice ages** when temperatures dropped and parts of the earth froze over. Today, the majority of scientists agree that the air around the earth—its **atmosphere**—is getting warmer. Human actions, such as the burning of fossil fuels for energy (see p. 48), which gives out harmful gases, are part of the reason for the rise in the atmosphere's temperature, known as global warming.

WHO WAS ARRHENIUS?

Svante Arrhenius (1859–1927) was a Swedish scientist who was the first person to calculate the effect of humans adding carbon dioxide to the atmosphere.

WIND

Winds can be incredibly strong, sometimes even enough to rip trees from the ground. Wind is all about **air pressure**—how much air is pressing down on the earth's surface. Air rushes from areas of high pressure to areas of low pressure—we call this wind.

sun

warm air over land

cool air over land

wind direction

high pressure   low pressure

TRY THIS AT HOME

BUILD YOUR OWN WIND VANE

The wind often changes direction. You can keep track of these movements by building your very own wind vane.

YOU WILL NEED:

✔ An adult helper
✔ A paper coffee cup with a lid
✔ A pencil with an eraser tip
✔ A straw (if it's a bendy one cut the bendy part off)

✔ Some stones
✔ Scissors
✔ Cardstock
✔ A pin
✔ A compass
✔ A marker

1 Cut out an arrowhead (a triangle) and a square from the cardstock.

2 Cut a 1-cm slit in the ends of the straw, and slot the shapes into the slits.

3 Fill the cup with stones, put the lid on, and turn it upside down.

4 Stick the pencil through the base of the upturned cup.

5 Carefully, poke the pin through the middle of the straw and into the eraser. Ask an adult to help you.

6 Use your compass (see p. 43) to find North, South, East, and West, and write N, S, E, and W on the sides of the cup.

7 Watch as the wind vane turns in the wind. How often does it change? In which direction does it blow most often?

N

THE MOON

The moon circles around the earth once a month. It is the brightest object in the night sky because it is the closest to us. It reflects light from the sun toward us like a giant space mirror.

what's the BIG idea?

MOON PHASES

The moon appears to change shape in the sky. Sometimes we see a full moon, sometimes a half moon, and sometimes a crescent. It hasn't really changed shape. When the moon is between the earth and the sun , the side facing us is dark. As the moon moves, we see more of it lit up.

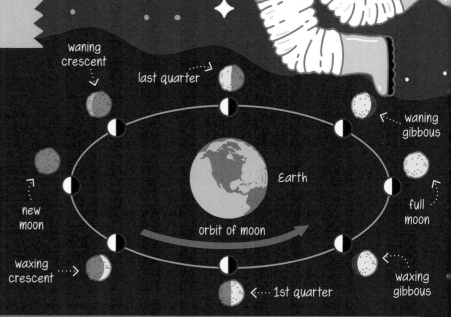

waning crescent

last quarter

waning gibbous

new moon

Earth

full moon

orbit of moon

light from the sun

waxing crescent

1st quarter

waxing gibbous

TRY THIS AT HOME

MOON DIARY

Keep an eye out for the moon in the sky. When you see it, sketch its shape and write down the date. Can you spot the pattern of the repeating phases?

MAKE YOUR OWN CRATERS

If you look at the moon through a pair of binoculars or through a telescope you will see that it is covered in lots of holes called craters. They were formed when **asteroids** and **comets** crashed into the moon and exploded on impact. In this fun experiment, you're going to make your own craters!

YOU WILL NEED:

✔ A deep plastic tray (or baking dish)

✔ Enough flour to fill the tray

✔ Cocoa powder

✔ Marbles of different sizes

✔ A magnifying glass

1. Fill the tray with flour. Use your hands or the back of a spoon to pack it in tightly to get as much flour in there as possible.

2. Sprinkle a layer of cocoa powder over the top of the flour so that you can no longer see it.

3. Drop a marble from a good height into the tray. What happens?

4. Try experimenting with different-sized marbles dropped from different heights or thrown at different angles. You can always fill your craters in if you run out of room. Do you notice any patterns? Check with your magnifying glass.

HOW DOES IT WORK?

Look closely at the craters you made. Can you see any rays shooting out from the holes like spokes on a wheel? You can also spot these "ray craters" on the moon with a pair of binoculars.

WHO WAS GALILEO?

Galileo Galilei (1564—1642) was an Italian astronomer (a scientist who studies the universe) who was one of the first to point a telescope at the moon. He saw craters and mountains and worked out their height by studying the shadows.

63

THE PLANETS

We live in a solar system filled with at least eight very different planets. Some are small and rocky like Earth, but others are huge and made of gas like Jupiter.

what's the BIG idea?

A LIVING PLANET

Earth is the only planet in our **solar system** known to have life. Scientists think that's because of its water. Earth has water because it's positioned at just the right distance from the sun. It's not too hot nor too cold, but just right! In 2015, an orbiter exploring Earth's neighboring planet, Mars, discovered dark stains on cliffs that might have once been water. Did Mars once have life, too?

too hot   just right   too cold

Venus

Mars

SUN

Mercury   Earth   Jupiter

IN FACT...

PLANET GAZING

You don't need a telescope to see some of the planets. Mercury, Venus, Mars, Jupiter, and Saturn, are all bright enough to be seen with your own eyes.

Venus

Mars

Uranus

Mercury

Earth   Jupiter   Saturn   Neptune

PUZZLE ZONE

MATCH THE ORBIT TO THE PLANET

Here's a list of the times it takes for the eight known planets to orbit the sun. Can you match the time to the correct planet?

30,687 days, 687 days, 365 days, 60,190 days, 88 days, 225 days, 4,333 days, 10,756 days

ANSWERS ARE AT THE BACK OF THE BOOK

Johannes Kepler (1571–1630) was a German mathematician who was the first to work out the rules by which planets orbit the sun.

TRY THIS AT HOME

WHY DO PLANETS ORBIT?

Most of the planets have nearly circular orbits. How come they don't fly off into space or crash into the sun? You're going to pretend to be a planet and find out!

YOU WILL NEED:

✔ An adult helper

✔ A piece of rope at least 6 1/2 ft (2 m) long

✔ A large open space, such as a park

1 You are going to be a planet and your adult helper is going to be the sun. First, ask your adult helper to tie the rope around your waist.

2 Give the other end of the rope to your helper. He or she must hold on to it tightly.

3 Try to walk away from your helper in a straight line and at a right angle (90°).

4 If you keep trying to do this what happens?

HOW DOES IT WORK?

Planets want to move in a straight line. At the same time, the force of gravity between the planet and the sun (represented by the rope) is pulling the planet toward it. The result is that the planet takes a nearly circular path around the sun.

THE SUN

The sun fills up the day with light and gives us the warmth and energy we need to survive. Scientists, we wouldn't be here without the sun!

WHAT'S GOING ON?

THE SUN'S ENERGY SOURCE

In our solar system (the sun and the planets around it), the sun is the only object that makes its own light. It can do this because the temperature at the center of the sun is a whopping 27 million °F (15 million °C). That's hot enough for a process called nuclear fusion to take place. In nuclear fusion, atomic nuclei fuse (join) creating vast amounts of energy. This is what makes the sun and other stars shine.

nuclear fusion takes place in the core

energy radiates out

SUN

WHO WAS BETHE?

Hans Bethe (1906–2005) was a German physicist who researched nuclear fusion and won the Nobel Prize for Physics in 1967.

IN FACT...

WHAT IS THE SUN MADE OF?

The sun is made mostly of two gases—hydrogen and helium. We get the word helium from the Greek word for the sun, because helium gas was found in the sun (in 1868) before it was discovered on Earth (in 1882).

MAKE YOUR OWN SUNDIAL

Long before we had electronic watches and phones, our ancestors used the sun to keep the time. Every day the sun appears to move across the sky, and so an object's shadow also seems to move. Make this sundial to see how that moving shadow acts like the hand of a clock.

YOU WILL NEED:

- ✔ A paper plate
- ✔ A straw
- ✔ Colored pencils

1 Use a pencil to make a hole through the center of the plate.

2 Poke the straw through the hole.

3 Write the number 12 at the top of the plate and bend your straw slightly toward it.

12

4 Go outside on a sunny day at midday, and place your sundial on the ground so that the shadow of the straw lines up with the number 12.

5 Come back after an hour and write the number 1 next to the shadow.

6 Repeat each hour until you have the rest of the afternoon numbers.

7 Where do you think the shadow will be the next morning? Fill in the numbers there, too.

IN FACT...

EARTH'S ROTATION

The sun doesn't really move across the sky. It only seems to move because the earth rotates. It takes 24 hours for the earth to spin once, so it takes that long for the sun to return to the same spot. It takes 365 days (one year) for the earth to complete an orbit of the sun.

THE STARS

On a dark night, far from the bright lights of a city, you should be able to see up to three thousand stars twinkling away at you. They are just like the sun but very far away.

WHAT'S GOING ON?

WHY DO STARS TWINKLE?

The stars only twinkle because you are looking at them through the layers of gases around the earth, known as the atmosphere. If you were in space, or somewhere with no atmosphere like the moon, you wouldn't see the stars twinkle at all.

IN FACT...

DISTANCES TO THE STARS

Our nearest star (after the sun) is called Proxima Centauri. It is a staggering 25 trillion miles (40 trillion km) away! Rather than use these big numbers, astronomers often use light years instead—the distance light travels in a year. A light year is about 6 trillion miles (9.5 trillion km)! Proxima Centauri is 4.2 light years away.

WHO WAS PAYNE?

Cecilia Payne (1900–1979) was an English astronomer who discovered that stars are mainly made of hydrogen and helium, and that they can be grouped according to their temperatures.

SPOT A CONSTELLATION

Thousands of years ago, our ancestors noticed how stars formed patterns and shapes. They played a giant game of dot-to-dot and connected the stars into shapes called **constellations**. Modern astronomers recognize 88 constellations. Can you spot these famous star patterns?

LOOK UP AT THE NIGHT SKY!

1 Orion (hunter) is most visible October–February.

2 Leo (lion) is most visible March–June.

3 Cygnus (swan) is most visible July–September.

IN FACT...

STAR TYPES AND THE BRIGHTNESS OF STARS

Stars come in seven different types depending on their size and temperature. These types are given the letters O, B, A, F, G, K, M. The sun is a G type star. The bigger the star, the hotter it is and the shorter its lifetime.

If you look up at the stars you'll notice that some are brighter than others. Astronomers have a word for the brightness of a star: magnitude. The lower the number, the brighter or more luminous the star. The brightest star in the night sky—Sirius—is so dazzling that it has a negative magnitude (−1.46).

STAR COLORS

Next time there is a clear night, look up at the stars and see if you can spot any stars that are red. These stars are dying and getting bigger over time. One day they will explode in a violent event called a supernova!

THE CHEMISTRY OF YOU

Some of the most interesting chemistry occurring around us is happening right inside our bodies. Biochemistry is the study of chemistry inside living things.

what's the BIG idea?

HORMONES

Throughout your body you have small organs called glands. Your glands make chemicals called hormones, which they send out into your body to do special jobs. The pancreas, for example, creates the hormone insulin, which helps manage the amount of glucose in your blood.

WHAT'S GOING ON?

ENZYMES

Enzymes are molecules in your body that help important chemical reactions occur. Scientists say they are **catalysts**. Catalysts are substances that change the speed of a chemical reaction while staying the same themselves. A great example is your saliva. Your saliva contains an enzyme called amylase that helps to break down food for digestion.

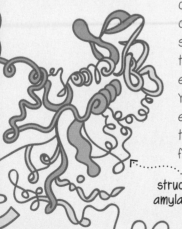

structure of an amylase enzyme

THE INSULIN HORMONE

If you have too much glucose in your blood after eating, your pancreas secretes insulin into your blood.

Pancreas secretes insulin into your bloodstream

Insulin causes glucose to move from blood into your cells

WHO WAS SOHONIE?

Kamala Sohonie (1912–1998) was an Indian biochemist who worked on the study of enzymes. She was the first Indian woman to get a Ph.D. in science.

DNA BASES

The double helix structure of DNA (right) is made from four smaller chemical building blocks that biochemists call nucleotide bases. They are adenine (A), cytosine (C), guanine (G), and thymine (T).

adenine   thymine

guanine   cytosine

EXTRACT DNA FROM A BANANA

You don't need a fancy, expensive laboratory to experiment with DNA. You can remove the DNA from a banana using these steps!

YOU WILL NEED:

✔ A ripe, peeled banana
✔ A resealable zip-lock bag
✔ Hot water
✔ Salt
✔ Dishwashing liquid
✔ Rubbing alcohol
✔ Filter paper or coffee filter
✔ A tall glass
✔ A wooden ice cream stick / coffee stirrer

1 Place the rubbing alcohol in the freezer a few minutes ahead of time.

2 Add half the banana to the bag, seal, and mash up into a paste.

rubbing alcohol

3 Add a teaspoon of salt to ½ cup of hot water, and add this to the bag.

4 Close the bag and gently massage it to mix the water into the banana.

5 Add ½ teaspoon of dishwashing liquid to the bag and gently mix.

6 Pour contents of the bag through the filter paper into the glass. Throw the paper away.

7 Tip the glass to one side, and slowly drip the rubbing alcohol down the inside of the glass until it forms a layer on top of the liquid at least ³/₄ in (2 cm) thick.

8 Wait 10 minutes.

9 Can you see some cloudy, white stuff moving around inside the alcohol? That's banana DNA!

REMARKABLE BIOMEDICINE

In many parts of the world, people are living longer and fewer people are dying young from diseases. That's thanks to scientific research, which discovers new ways to find and treat medical problems.

what's the BIG idea?

ANTIBIOTICS

Many nasty conditions are caused by infections of bacteria. Antibiotics are drugs that kill bacteria or stop them from reproducing. Antibiotics have had a big positive effect on global health over the last century.

WHO WAS FLEMING?

Alexander Fleming (1881–1955) was a Scottish biologist who discovered penicillin—the world's first human-made antibiotic—in 1928.

WHAT'S GOING ON?

ANTIBIOTIC RESISTANCE

Largely due to the overuse of antibiotics, bacteria are developing resistance to our most powerful drugs (see p. 23), which means they are not killed off so easily. So, scientists are researching new antibiotics by taking examples from nature. Leafcutter ants, for instance, create their own antibiotics from bacteria in their surroundings.

MRI AND CT SCANS

Good medicine isn't just about treating a problem—it is also about figuring out what the problem is in the first place. Scientists have invented clever ways to look inside your body without surgery. These include Magnetic Resonance Imaging (MRI) (below) and Computerized Tomography (CT) scans.

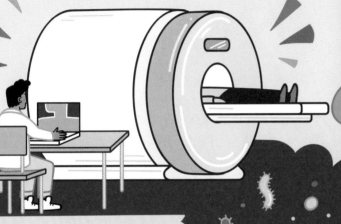

WHAT'S GOING ON?

NANOTECHNOLOGY

An exciting area of modern medicine is nanotechnology, which uses tiny materials that are too small for the human eye to see. One day tiny machines might be added to your body to hunt out and fix problems.

TRY THIS AT HOME

EXPERIMENTING WITH BACTERIA

Bacteria are all around us, all the time. There are as many bacteria inside you as there are your own cells. In this experiment, you'll cultivate the bacteria around you.

YOU WILL NEED:

✔ An adult helper
✔ A large potato
✔ A peeler
✔ A knife
✔ A pair of new rubber gloves
✔ Four zip-lock bags
✔ A marker

WARNING! SHARP KNIFE!

C BREATH FLOOR HANDS

1. Put on the gloves, and ask an adult to peel the potato and cut it into quarters.

2. Add one quarter to one of the zip-lock bags and seal. This is your control. Write "C" on the bag.

3. Blow and cough onto another piece of potato for several minutes. Add to a second bag and seal. Label it "Breath."

4. Rub a third piece of potato on the floor, add to a bag, seal, and write "Floor."

5. Remove the gloves, rub the last quarter in your hands for several minutes. Add to the final bag, seal, and label it "Hands."

6. Place all four bags in a dark place for one week.

7. Check the bags every day. Write down any changes to the potatoes. At the end of the week, which bag has changed most compared to the control? Can you think why that might be?

INCREDIBLE BIOTECHNOLOGY

Understanding how living things work has helped us to make changes that benefit society. Let's take a look!

➡ what's the BIG idea?

GENETICALLY MODIFIED (GM) FOODS

Scientists have been able to alter the genetic code of plants to change the way they behave. Some plants have been made resistant to insects, other pests, and disease. By making these changes in the plants' DNA, farmers don't have to spray the crops with pesticides (chemicals used to kill pests), which can be harmful to the environment. But we don't yet know if eating these GM crops causes harm to people.

WHO IS JAENISCH?

Rudolf Jaenisch (b. 1942) is an American biologist who was the first scientist to genetically modify an animal when he experimented with mice in 1974.

WHAT'S GOING ON?

➡ INSULIN PRODUCTION

People who have a disease called diabetes do not produce enough of the hormone insulin (see p. 70), so they need regular insulin injections. A long time ago, we had to get this insulin from the pancreas of pigs. But biotechnology changed that. Scientists have inserted the genetic code for making human insulin into bacteria, which now produce huge quantities to keep people with diabetes healthy.

human insulin gene

gene is inserted into DNA from bacteria

bacteria starts to produce insulin

what's the BIG idea?

CLONING

Cloning is when scientists make an exact genetic copy of something. This can be a single cell or a whole living thing. The clone has exactly the same DNA as the original. In the 1990s, Dolly the Sheep was the first clone of an adult mammal.

WHO WAS HALDANE?

J.B.S. Haldane (1892–1964) was a British-Indian biologist who, in 1963, first used the word "clone."

TRY THIS AT HOME

BIOTECHNOLOGY— GOOD OR BAD?

Another example of biotechnology is the making of the chemical ethanol by adding genetically modified bacteria to plant waste. Ethanol is used to make fuel and alcoholic drinks. This is quite a simple and common process, but not everyone is happy about the advances in some other types of biotechnology. Some people wonder if it is right to directly interfere with nature.

Talk to your family and teachers about the subject. What do they think? Search online for information about biotechnology. Use this research to write a list of what's good or not so good about biotechnology.

IN FACT...

STEM CELLS

Most cells have special jobs to do. But stem cells are those that don't yet have a job, and they can develop into many different types of cells. Scientists are working on cloning stem cells so they can be turned into specialized cells in order to treat a wide range of diseases.

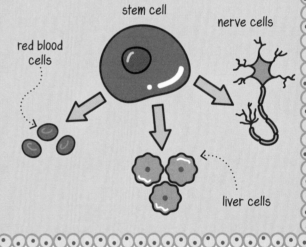

stem cell

nerve cells

red blood cells

liver cells

75

Glossary

ACID
A chemical that produces positively charged hydrogen ions when dissolved in water.

AIR PRESSURE
The "push" exerted by air as it presses against something.

ASTEROID
Small rocky or metal objects smaller than planets that orbit the sun.

ATOM
The building blocks of everything around us—they have a nucleus with orbiting electrons.

ATMOSPHERE
The layer of gases that surrounds a planet or moon.

BACTERIA
Tiny, single-celled organisms

BASE (AS IN ALKALI)
A chemical that produces negatively charged hydroxide ions (made of hydrogen and oxygen) when dissolved in water.

CARBON DIOXIDE
A gas made up of carbon and oxygen, chemically combined.

CELLS
The building blocks of which all living things are made.

CHARGE (AS IN POSITIVE OR NEGATIVE)
An electric charge that is the property of certain particles, including the electrons and the protons in atoms.

CHEMICAL REACTION
A process that reorganizes the atoms in substances, producing one or more new substances.

CLIMATE
A long-term pattern of weather, temperature, and atmospheric conditions.

COMET
An object made of dust, gas, and ice that orbits the sun. It's visible as a slow-moving point with a tail.

CONCENTRATION
The amount of a substance in a defined space. It's often considered the "strength" of a solution.

CONDENSATION
Drops of liquid that form on a cold surface as gas changes to liquid (condenses), and the process of this happening.

CONDENSE
To form as a liquid, from a gas.

CONSTELLATION
A group of stars that form a pattern and have been given a name, such as Orion.

CYTOPLASM
The fluid that fills the inside of a cell.

DENSITY
The mass of a substance relative to its volume—its compactness.

DEPOSITION
Changing straight from a gas to a solid without going through the liquid phase.

DNA (DEOXYRIBONUCLEIC ACID)
The chemical that makes up chromosomes. It carries the information that acts like a recipe for building and running a living thing.

DOUBLE HELIX
Two spiral shapes twisted together, as in DNA.

ELECTRICITY
Normally means an electric current, and most electric currents involve the movement of electrons in wires.

ELECTROMAGNETIC FORCE
The force that acts within atoms to keep electrons orbiting around the nucleus. It holds matter together.

ELECTRON
A tiny part of an atom that carries a small, negative electric charge. Electrons orbit the nucleus of an atom.

ENERGY
The property that makes it possible for objects or substances to do something, such as to move or to make heat.

ENVIRONMENT
The surroundings in which an organism lives.

EVAPORATION
The process of a liquid changing to a gas as it heats up.

EVOLUTION
The process by which living things change over time. Some types die out, others change, and new types develop.

FREEZING

The process of a liquid turning into a solid as a result of extreme cooling.

GENE

Part of a chromosome. Genes are the smallest part of the genetic "recipe" for making a living thing.

GRAVITY

The force that pulls objects toward each other. Gravity holds the moon close to Earth, and makes objects fall toward Earth's center.

HYDROGEN

A colorless, odorless gas that is the lightest of all elements.

ICE AGE

A period (sometimes lasting millions of years) when the earth's temperature drops and large areas are covered with ice.

INTESTINES (SMALL INTESTINE AND LARGE INTESTINE)

Organs in an animal or human, in which nutrients are absorbed from food.

KINETIC ENERGY

A type of energy that an object or particle has when it moves.

LENS

A curved piece of transparent material that can bend rays of light.

MATTER

Any substance that takes up space—whether solid, liquid, or gas.

MELTING

The process in which heat changes something from a solid to a liquid.

MEMBRANE

A very thin sheet or layer that often forms a boundary around a structure, such as the membrane around a cell.

MITOSIS

The process by which a cell divides, making two exact copies of itself.

MOLECULE

Two or more atoms joined by a chemical bond. A molecule can contain atoms of the same element or different elements.

MUTATION

A random change in the genetic code of a living thing that results from mistakes in copying the DNA in cells.

NATURAL SELECTION

The process behind evolution. Living things with characteristics that help them to survive in their environment are most likely to reproduce and pass on those characteristics.

NECTAR

A sweet, sugary liquid produced by flowering plants.

NEUTRON

A tiny particle in the nucleus of an atom that has neither a positive nor a negative electric charge.

NUCLEUS

The central part of an atom that contains the protons and neutrons. Also, the "control center" of a cell.

NUTRIENTS

A chemical that a living thing needs for nourishment, either to provide energy or to build its body.

OXYGEN

An element (and gas) essential to life that makes up about one-fifth of the earth's atmosphere.

PITCH

The highness or lowness of a sound, determined by its frequency (how rapidly its source is vibrating).

POLLEN

A powdery substance produced by flowering plants that causes a plant to form seeds.

POTENTIAL ENERGY

The energy bound up in an object that has the potential to be turned into other forms of energy.

PROTON

A tiny, positively charged particle often found in the nucleus of an atom.

REFRACTION

The bending of light when it moves between different transparent substances, such as glass and air.

REPRODUCE

To reproduce offspring (young).

RESISTANCE (AS IN AN ANTIBIOTIC)

The ability of bacteria to withstand the effects of antibiotic drugs so that they can reproduce.

RETINA

The layer of cells at the back of the eyeball that picks up light and sends electrical signals to the brain, allowing you to see.

SOLAR SYSTEM

The system of the sun, Earth, and other planets that orbit around it, including moons, comets, and asteroids.

SPECIES

A group of living things that have characteristics in common and that can breed to produce young.

TIDE

The movement of the sea caused by the pull of gravity from the moon and the sun.

VEINS

Blood vessels that carry blood back to the heart from the body.

PUZZLE ZONE ANSWERS

PAGES 22–23 ADAPTATION AND EVOLUTION

Adapting Animals

Camel — humps for fat storage

Giraffe — long neck to reach leaves

Chameleon — changes color to hide from predators and prey

Eagle — talons and beak to catch prey

Seal — thick coat for warmth

PAGES 64–65 PLANETS

Match the Orbit to the Planet

30,687 days: Uranus

687 days: Mars

365 days: Earth

60,190 days: Neptune

88 days: Mercury

225 days: Venus

4,333 days: Jupiter

10,756 days: Saturn

INDEX

Index entries in **bold** refer to experiments and projects